Problems of Plenty

PROBLEMS OF PLENTY

The American Farmer in the Twentieth Century

R. Douglas Hurt

The American Ways Series

IVAN R. DEE   *Chicago*

Library of Congress Cataloging-in-Publication Data:
Hurt, R. Douglas.
    Problems of plenty : the American farmer in the twentieth
century / R. Douglas Hurt.
        p. cm. — (The American ways series)
    Includes bibliographical references (p.   ).
    ISBN 1-56663-463-6 (cloth : alk. paper) — ISBN 1-56663-462-8
(paper : alk. paper)
    1. Agriculture—United States—History—20th century. 2.
Agriculture and state—United States—History—20th century. 3.
Agriculture—Economic aspects—United States—History—20th
century. I. Title. II. Series.

S441 .H925 2002
630'.973'0904—dc21   2002067431

For Mary Ellen, Adlai, and Austin

Contents

Preface

AMERICAN AGRICULTURE in the twentieth century is a story of abundant harvests, rapid technological and scientific change, and great prosperity. It is also a tale of desperate men and women, white and black, who struggled—often against overwhelming odds in the form of inadequate land, insufficient credit, and inequitable treatment—to make a living from the soil that would give them dignity and comfort. American agriculture in the twentieth century is also the story of great demographic change as farm men, women, and children moved from the countryside to towns and cities, seeking a better life. In this respect it is often the history of economic failure that spawned radical organizations and violence. Above all, however, American agriculture in the twentieth century is the story of farmers' dependency on the federal government.

When the century began, farmers looked to the federal government for information about how to become more productive. The government met this need in a limited fashion by disseminating research reports from the experiment stations and by hosting seminars, called farmers' institutes, at the land-grant colleges. There agriculturists were informed about improved methods, seeds, and livestock. This work expanded notably with the passage of the Smith-Lever Act in 1914, which authorized county and home demonstration agents to help make farm men and women more productive and efficient and thereby increase their profits and improve their standard of living. As a result, farmers began to depend on the federal government for technical advice.

During the Progressive Era, farmers also looked to the federal government to bring abusive corporate practices under control as well as help them compete effectively in the marketplace. They needed better access to credit and, in the business world, regulatory practices that favored farmers. Economic recession soon encouraged farmers to seek new forms of aid from the federal government, particularly in the marketing of their products and in price supports. During the Great Depression the price- and income-support and acreage-reduction programs of the Roosevelt administration were forced on farmers in hopes that direct economic relief would stimulate the farm economy. If the purchasing power of farmers could be increased, it was thought, this would stimulate manufacturing and industrial production, and the domestic economy would improve. Dramatic scientific and technological change, however, continued to make farmers more productive, despite government attempts to limit production. As a result, farmers came to depend on the federal government for price-support programs that would enable them to earn a living comparable to the nonfarm population. Government economic aid would also help farmers remain on the land even though they continued to produce price-depressing surpluses of many staple crops such as cotton, wheat, and rice, and dairy products. By the late twentieth century this dependency was not only willful but long established. Farmers considered federal aid—in the form of price-supporting loans and acreage-reduction payments—nothing less than an entitlement. By the turn of the twenty-first century, farmers remained even more dependent on the federal government after a failed attempt to free them from economic support was replaced by a return to income support through direct payments for participation in commodity-reduction and environmental programs.

Although the history of American agricultural policy is complex, often confusing, and sometimes contradictory, this book provides a brief and broad survey of the major policy developments that affected farm men and women in the twentieth century. Several themes recur. First, federal aid, intervention, and regulation in agriculture occurred persistently and in many forms. Second, since the 1920s government economic aid through a number of programs and formulas failed to stabilize agricultural production and markets and shield farmers from the "cost-price squeeze." Third, with the exception of the 1930s, the farm population fell while individual farms grew larger. Fourth, farmers were unable to unify in a single organization that would speak for agriculture with one voice—regional and commodity interests have been too diffuse. Fifth, Congress, the U.S. Department of Agriculture, the extension service, and land-grant colleges acted on the premise that farmers needed technical and economic aid and that government could improve agricultural life not only for the benefit of farm men, women, and children but also to ensure a healthy national economy and an abundant food supply.

No "typical" farm characterized American agriculture in the twentieth century. Farmers grew more specialized, emphasizing crops or livestock such as corn, soybeans, and hogs in the Midwest; dairying in New England; cotton and tobacco and later soybeans and cattle in the South; vegetables, fruits, cotton, and rice in California; wheat in the Pacific Northwest; and cattle on ranges leased from the federal government in the Mountain West. Since no typical farm existed, there was no "typical" farmer in the twentieth century. Because this book emphasizes agricultural policy, however, I am concerned chiefly with farmers who participated in government production-control programs. These programs emphasized staple crops or commodities that could be stored for long periods of time, because storage enables the government to purchase designated surplus commodities and keep them off the market in order to prevent unacceptably low prices. As a result, the term *farmer* used in this book refers primarily to those staple commodity producers who looked to the federal government for economic support in the form of production control, marketing aid, price-supporting loans, and direct income payments. Still, nothing about agriculture is simple in a market economy. Even by emphasizing agricultural policy in a context of regulation and dependency, the history of farm policy is complex, and is rife with false starts and diversions.

This short history, then, is the story of how farmers came to depend on the federal government in the twentieth century. Although I discuss scientific and technological change, organizations, and economic affairs, among other matters, I do so in relation to the changes in agriculture that prompted farmers to seek government support for survival. They wanted to improve their agricultural practices and thereby their standard of living, and to gain sufficient income to remain on the land. In each case their dependency was based on the power of the federal government to regulate business, credit institutions, and corporations as well as to design policies that provided direct cash income to farmers for participating in a variety of programs.

I am grateful to John Braeman, editor of the American Ways Series, for inviting me to write this book and for the opportunity to reach students and general readers who are interested in American agricultural history, particularly farm policy. George McJimsey and David Hamilton provided excellent suggestions and crucial advice for improving the manuscript, and I will be forever thankful for their time and generosity. Over the years I have had the opportunity to work with many students who have helped me learn about American agricultural history. Jim Chrisinger especially enhanced my knowledge about the grain embargo during the Carter administration. Moreover, every synthesis depends on the quality of the work that has preceded it. I am fortunate that the historians who have written about American agricultural history in the twentieth century have provided a rich body of literature for study and learning. The Note on Sources at the end of this book reflects only a portion of their contribution to the field and their influence on my own work.

R. D. H.

Ames, Iowa
June 2002

big market
producers
needed a bailout
just like any
other US industry

Problems of Plenty

1

The Progressive Era

THE TWENTIETH CENTURY dawned with promise and opportunity for American farm men and women on the "last great frontier," where cheap lands and speculators lured homesteaders to the northern Great Plains. Between 1900 and 1915 some 100,000 newcomers settled beyond the Missouri River in South Dakota, an area known as the "West River Country." For anyone still to speak of an agricultural frontier, however, reflected a remarkable ignorance about farming not only in the Great Plains but also about a national economy increasingly driven and identified by cities, factories, wage earners, and machines. In 1900 most Americans were not farmers, nor had they been for approximately a quarter-century. As each decade passed, fewer still wanted to farm.* Those who remained on the land increasingly looked to government, both federal and state, to aid their income and way of life. For some, however, the spirit of independence created by the lure of cheap lands, relatively accessible by railroad, proved irresistible. They saw an opportunity to improve their lives

---

*The census of 1920 showed that the rural population declined to less than half of the total population. But rural people are not necessarily agricultural people. Sometime between the 1870 and 1880 census, the agricultural population fell below half of the general population.

through agriculture in a land of searing sun, bitter cold, and little rain.

The settlement of the last great frontier, as some called it, began in 1904 when the General Land Office announced the opening of surplus lands on the Rosebud Reservation in South Dakota for settlement by whites. The federal government required that individuals apply in person at four designated towns to qualify for the lottery that would provide homesteads for 2,412 settlers. More than 106,000 applicants registered for the lottery. In contrast to the homesteaders of the late nineteenth century, settlers could not claim these lands free of charge. Lottery lands cost as much as four dollars per acre, but settlers could pay for the land over five years. Or they could "commute"—that is, pay the entire amount after fourteen months and receive title to the land. Four years later the federal government opened an additional 4,000 claims on the reservation that drew nearly 114,800 applicants. The General Land Office offered additional homesteading tracts in western South Dakota until 1915.

The homesteaders who ventured onto the northern Great Plains during the early twentieth century proved as little prepared for farming in the region as the generation that had preceded them in the late nineteenth century, and many failed. Even so, a spirit of incredible optimism prevailed among them, not simply about the importance of land ownership for ensuring wealth and security but of farming as enabling a free and independent life. One seasoned reporter covering the opening of the Rosebud Reservation for the *American Mercury* in 1908, swept up in the exuberance of the moment, concluded that the men and women who settled this last great frontier proved that the "best that was in our fathers . . . is with us yet." Although these settlers clung to the Jeffersonian ideal that championed the small-scale farmer as the foundation of the national economy and democracy, that ideal by the turn of the twentieth century lived in the minds of most farmers only as a myth. The economic need to specialize in one-crop agriculture in a market economy dictated their daily lives, which were now influenced, if not controlled, as much by creditors, processors, foreign buyers, and international exchange rates as by the weather.

While homesteaders in the northern Great Plains exemplified the optimism of the past in American agriculture, the rural South remained locked in an agricultural system that epitomized degradation, poverty, and want. At the beginning of the twentieth century, Southern agriculture adhered to the traditions of a bygone age. The South was not a land of prosperous, independent, landowning farmers. Tenancy and sharecropping remained a way of life in Southern agriculture, and both encompassed an increasing proportion of the agricultural population.

By 1900 nearly half of Southern farms were operated by nonowners. White planters, who owned considerable acreage but who had little capital to hire labor, entered into a variety of labor agreements whereby they contracted with white and black farmers to work their lands as either sharecroppers or tenants. In this way the planters could divide their large landholdings into small farms of fewer than fifty acres. In the absence of a sound banking system and other credit institutions, small-scale and often landless Southern farmers could not obtain the financing they needed to buy seed, implements, and mules as well as manufactured goods for daily living until they harvested and sold their cotton and tobacco crops. Thus the planters or large-scale landowners and merchants met this need by providing credit or by financing their tenants' farming operations. This credit, however, was not monetary, in the form of a cash advance. Instead the planter and sharecropper usually entered into an oral contract by which the landowner agreed to provide a house, land, equipment, seed, fertilizer, and a mule as well as the bare necessities of life called the "furnish," such as clothing, cornmeal, fat pork, and molasses, for the farm family during the year. In return the sharecropper agreed to farm the land as directed; at the end of the year the planter would divide the crop with him, less expenses. In essence the planter paid the sharecropper half the crop for the labor of his family during the year. Tenants brought more to the contractual arrangement than their labor. If they owned a mule and implements, for example, they might be classified as a "share tenant." They controlled ownership of the crop and paid the planter from a quarter to a third of the crop. If they also had money, they could contract to be a "cash renter" and keep the entire crop.

Lien laws gave the landlord or a local furnishing merchant the right to claim the sharecropper's crop. Essentially the sharecropper mortgaged his unplanted crop in January in order to be furnished until the settling of the harvest accounts in December. Almost invariably he drew more from the accounts of the landlord or furnishing merchant than his share of the cotton crop could repay. As a result, he became bound by a continuing contract, which further burdened him with debt and a loss of freedom. At the turn of the twentieth century, approximately 33 percent of all white farmers and 75 percent of all black farmers in the South were tenants or sharecroppers.

Southern agriculture and the economy of the region depended on cotton—production, ginning, marketing, shipping, and manufacture. The trinity of cotton, tenancy, and poverty ruled the lives of most Southern farmers. One observer called cotton the "white plague" and wrote that "Cotton is not only king; it is tyrant, and the people of the South, old and young, are its slaves." Cotton remained a labor-intensive crop, its cultivation little changed since the early nineteenth century. It demanded almost year-round labor, determined by the rhythms of the seasons which bound farm men, women, and children, black and white, to what one Southern writer called the "relentless tyranny of the soil." The crop left them little time, energy, or money for anything else. Plowing the land for planting occurred in late winter. Spring brought planting time; summer meant several cultivations with a mule and shovel plow or "chopping" cotton—that is, the weeds—with a hoe. Late autumn brought the harvest, which customarily required farmers to pick their fields three times because the bolls did not ripen uniformly. Cotton picking often left the fingers rough and raw. Skilled pickers knew they could ease their burden by picking the bolls at the bottom of the plant first. That would get the necessary back-aching stoop work out of the way early. This outlook indicated far more than a practical application of technique to the cotton harvest; it also suggested that tenants and sharecroppers had little to anticipate in life, including any hope of making enough money to rise out of debt and poverty.

In 1900 cotton determined the Southern economy because planters would not allow their tenants and sharecroppers to diversify by raising other crops and livestock. At even the low price of ten cents per pound in 1903, most planters continued to require their sharecroppers to raise cotton because it provided the greatest profits. Cotton did not spoil in storage, and markets always existed; diversification, on the other hand, required credit as well as technological, marketing, and storage changes that necessitated more capital than the planters commanded. Consequently they continued the safe, conservative ways of the past. Because of the emphasis on cotton, and in some areas tobacco, sharecroppers and tenants could not produce sufficient food for their families, and planters often prohibited them from planting anything other than the chief cash crop for their area. As a result they often suffered from malnutrition and pellagra. With an average family cultivating ap-

proximately twenty acres of cotton with one mule, they produced about two hundred pounds per acre. At ten cents per
pound, the crop earned $400, of which they received half, less
expenses. If they had any money at the end of the year they
were fortunate; usually they ended each year in deeper debt.
Without access to capital and reasonable credit, sharecroppers
could not break the bonds of obligation and indebtedness to
the planters and furnishing merchants. For the poor, dependency characterized their relationship with the landowning or
planter class.

Outside the South, farmers experienced relative prosperity
during the first two decades of the twentieth century. In New
England and the Middle Atlantic states, farmers continued to
emphasize dairying and the production of fruits and vegetables. Urban populations created a demand for fluid milk,
which brought high prices and greater profits than grain and
livestock. Farmers in Maine's Aroostook Valley became
known for their production of potatoes; agriculturists in New
Jersey and Delaware produced eggs, poultry, and truck crops;
many farmers in New York and Connecticut raised apples and
peaches. The prosperity of Northern farmers, however, was
most evident in the Midwest.* In 1900 the Midwest served as
the breadbasket of the nation, producing wheat, corn, cattle,
hogs, and dairy products. Here too farmers specialized, some
producing corn to sell or feed to livestock, while others emphasized wheat and still others beef and dairy cattle. In every
case these farmers produced for the market, that is, to make
money. Midwestern farms tended to be single-family operations. The head of the household owned or rented the land
and worked it with the help of his wife and children. Because

---

*Here I use the U.S. Bureau of Census definition of the Midwest, which
includes Ohio, Indiana, Illinois, Michigan, Wisconsin, Minnesota, Iowa,
Nebraska, North Dakota, South Dakota, and Kansas. I do not, however, include Missouri, which arguably is more a Southern than a
Northern state, culturally and historically.

farmers seldom paid themselves a wage, they absorbed or ignored their labor costs, which in turn helped them earn a profit. New and improved implements, however, steadily reduced the need for large families and hired labor. A boy, a binder, and four horses, for example, could cut as much wheat in a day as ten to fifteen men had done in 1850. Higher wages and shorter hours in city jobs lured thousands of young men and women from Midwestern farms each year. But most of those who stayed remained optimistic about the future.

In the West by the turn of the twentieth century, California had become the major agricultural state. Although large-scale "bonanza" wheat farms characterized the commercial agriculture of California in the late nineteenth century, during the first decade of the new century irrigated fruits and vegetables for nearby urban populations offered the highest profits. Growers in southern California and the Central Valley also used refrigerated railway cars and cooperative marketing to reach Eastern markets. Large-scale landholdings, irrigation, and efficient transportation enabled farmers to specialize. But small-scale, diversified farmers often could not compete. Frequently they sold out to the large-scale growers who continued to acquire and consolidate their holdings. State irrigation policy made water cheap and accessible. California's specialty crop growers also depended on cheap temporary, migrant labor, particularly Japanese, Filipino, and Mexican. Racism drove the Japanese from the vegetable fields, vineyards, and orchards by 1920, and growers increasingly turned to Mexicans and Mexican-Americans who worked hard and did not attempt to unionize. The growers would continue to depend on cheap water and migrant labor for the remainder of the century.

In 1900, despite increasing specialization and consolidation, nearly 30 million people, or 42 percent of the U.S. population, still lived on 5.7 million farms. With the smallest farms in the Northeast and the South and the largest in the Midwest and

Far West, the average farm was about 147 acres, with approximately 50 acres improved—that is, cultivated and used for crops. About one-third of the American labor force worked in agriculturally related employment. Farmers produced more corn than any other commodity, but most of it reached the market as beef, pork, or poultry at the local butcher or grocery store. Wheat and cotton were the two major cash and export crops. In every region except the South, most farmers prospered. During the first two decades of the twentieth century, farm income doubled and the value of the average farm tripled.

Technological change particularly helped grain farmers increase their production through tilling, planting, and harvesting more acres. In the first two decades of the twentieth century, the gasoline-powered tractor became the most important new tool for farmers. But they did not rush to purchase these internal-combustion implements because early tractors were unreliable, expensive, and gigantic, much like large steam traction engines, which proved difficult to maneuver and required large acreage for operation. In 1917, however, Henry Ford developed a small, lightweight, low-cost tractor that could pull two plows. Known as the Fordson, it sold for about $750 and achieved immediate success after World War I because it met the power and labor needs of smaller-scale farmers. Still, most farmers preferred horses because of lower cost and because the Fordson was designed only for plowing and for powering threshing machinery rather than for cultivating row crops. By 1920 only 3.6 percent of farmers nationwide owned tractors.

No matter whether a farmer owned a tractor or even a steam engine, the rhythm of the seasons shaped farm life during the early twentieth century. Despite considerable technological change that eased their labor, farmers still relied primarily on skilled hands and horsepower. Farm men and women worked long hours to produce cash crops for domestic and world markets. They were commercial farmers—that is, they raised crops and livestock for profit to pay mortgages, purchase machinery, and buy clothes and groceries. At the turn of the twentieth century farm men and women still raised poultry, milked cows, and produced fruits and vegetables for their family table. But most were not subsistence or even self-sufficient farmers, nor did they want to be. *evidence*

At the same time the American tradition of landownership produced scattered and often isolated farm families. The U.S. Department of Agriculture (USDA) served farmers primarily through programs at land-grant colleges and in the experiment station system by supporting research to help make them more efficient and productive. The agency's regulatory duties mainly involved imposing quarantines for livestock. Most farmers never saw an agent from the USDA. The only government official that regularly touched their lives was the rural route mail carrier after Congress established that service on a permanent basis in 1902. Consequently the family was the primary economic, social, and educational institution in American agriculture and the countryside.

But many farmers were coming to believe that only the federal government could regulate the economy so as to allow agriculturists to share the wealth of the nation. Although the Populist movement had died, many farmers still believed that the federal government should regulate the railroads, agricultural credit, parcel post, and good roads to improve farm life for the good of the rural community and nation. In the first two decades of the twentieth century, characterized as the Progressive Era, and particularly in the years of the Wilson administration (1913–1921), farm-state lawmakers aided farmers to an unprecedented degree. They laid the foundations for the regulatory state in American agriculture.

how does this jive w/ Baron?

THE AGE OF PROSPERITY

Farmers acknowledged that agricultural life had improved because of new technology that made their work easier and more productive. Nor could they deny that, compared to the late nineteenth century, the prices they received for their commodities now exceeded their average expenditures. In 1900, for example, based on a farm price index of 100 for the period 1910–1914, farmers received an index price of 69 for their commodities. Those prices increased to 104 in 1910 and then jumped to 217 in 1919 as a result of wartime demand before falling to 211 the next year. At the same time the prices of farm products rose faster than the prices farmers paid for most of what they bought. In 1910 farmers paid an index price of 97 for production costs, including interest, taxes, and wages. The price relationship between farm and nonfarm products became so favorable to farmers that the period from 1909 to 1914 became the base period used to judge the fairness of agricultural prices in terms of "parity," that is, when the comparative purchasing power of farmers to nonfarmers was about equal.

Farmers received favorable prices because production had increased less than urban demands for food. Between 1900 and 1920 agricultural production rose by 30 percent while the national population increased 40 percent. As a result, agricultural prices—the prices paid to farmers—increased faster than the cost of other goods, and farmers prospered accordingly. Between 1910 and 1920 the average income per farm increased from $652 to $1,196. As agricultural income improved, land prices also rose, often doubling or tripling in value. Large capital gains based on land (at least on paper) enabled farmers to offer more collateral for loans, and farm debt began to increase significantly. By 1920 farmers' debt more than doubled, from $3.2 billion in 1910 to $8.4 billion. As long as agricultural com-

borrow more money based on land value

modity prices remained high, farmers could meet their mortgage payments and monthly bills for buying new tractors, threshing machines, and land, and they enjoyed a higher standard of living than ever before. Some observers see the first two decades of the twentieth century as a "golden age" for American farmers. By 1920, 30 percent of them owned automobiles, chiefly Henry Ford's Model T. European markets also improved, particularly during the war years from 1914 to 1918.

food needs

Higher agricultural prices encouraged farm men and women to specialize their production and participate in the market economy. By so doing, however, they grew more dependent on others. In 1900, for example, the average farm family produced 60 percent of its food needs; in 1920 it produced only 40 percent. By the end of the Progressive Era, most farmers bought most of their food at local grocery stores, and the farm population continued to decline, falling to 30 percent of the national population, though the number of farms remained about the same at 6.4 million, averaging 149 acres. In the towns and cities, employment opportunities that paid more money for fewer hours of work lured men and women who wished to improve their standard of living and leave their often isolated homes in the countryside. Fewer men and women also chose to remain on their farms for the same reasons that their sons and daughters often moved away.

how do you find this stat?

Even during this period of relative prosperity, some farmers complained that they had no control over marketing and prices because they sold wholesale and bought retail. Since they could not control production, they could not control prices like the large grain and meatpacking companies did. Such complaints remained muted so long as prices stayed high. Before the collapse in mid-1920, gross farm income reached a high of $17.9 billion. Land values had increased 190 percent in many areas.

But when agricultural prices fell to an index of 124 by 1921, while production costs rose to 155, farmers quickly turned to the federal government. They sought help far beyond the dissemination of agricultural knowledge to improve production. In so doing they turned their backs on the ideal of self-reliance in exchange for the security of an adequate standard of living.

bail-out

THE COUNTRY LIFE MOVEMENT

Despite the general farm prosperity of the early twentieth century, many urban reformers (educators, ministers, philosophers, and social scientists) believed that agriculture was backward. In their view, farmers had to become more efficient and their social and cultural lives more rewarding in order that men and women would stay on the farm—for their own good and for the benefit of the nation. Reformers also wanted a cheap and plentiful food supply for city dwellers. President Theodore Roosevelt declared that "Successful manufacturing depends primarily on cheap food." Urban reformers also believed that the countryside could provide a model for solving the problems of industrial America. They idealized farm life, arguing that country men and women were "frank, virile, direct, clean [and] independent."

Indeed, by the early twentieth century many Americans still believed that the cities existed only because of prosperous farms, where a special people worked the land with a God-given integrity that made them the protectors of the nation, the voice of democracy, and the foundation of national virtue. Much like J. Hector St. John de Crèvecoeur and Thomas Jefferson, modern intellectuals and reformers attributed the prosperity of American agriculture to the fertility of the land and the industry of the men and women who cultivated the fields. Their reward was prosperity, independence, and self-reliance, which in turn produced an egalitarian society and a

natural aristocracy based on character, integrity, and democratic government. Most rural people believed that farmers
were superior physically, intellectually, and morally to city
people. By farming their own land, men and women gained
strength of character and a strong moral commitment to education and social progress.

Urban reformers did not necessarily agree that country people were superior to city dwellers, but they did believe that
rural life needed social and economic improvement to ensure
the prosperity of the cities as well as enhance the lives of farm
men, women, and children. In 1907 President Roosevelt aided
the movement to reform and improve farm life when he appointed a Commission on Country Life to study the problems
of rural America, particularly on the farms. Roosevelt explained that the "problem of country life is in the truest sense
a national problem." Liberty Hyde Bailey, a horticulturist at
Cornell University and chairman of the Country Life Commission, which Roosevelt charged with making recommenda-
tions to improve farm life, also accepted the belief that
agrarian life was best for individuals and the nation. Bailey
contended that the city was like a parasite that ran its roots
into open country, draining rural life of its energy and sub-
stance. Several years later he wrote: "The city is elaborate and
artificial: the country is direct and natural." In contrast, to the
city, the farm was the foundation of the nation's morality as
well as the source of all national wealth. Without farmers,
America's agrarian values would perish. Improving farm life
would improve urban life.   connection btwn urban-
                                                          rural
When the Country Life Commission reported its findings
in January 1909, it concluded: "The underlying problem is to
develop and maintain on our farms a civilization in full har-
mony with the best American ideals. To build up and retain
this civilization means first of all that the business of agriculture must be made to yield a reasonable return to those who

be made?

follow it intelligently; and life on the farm must be made per-
manently satisfying to intelligent progressive people. The
work before us, therefore, is nothing more or less than the
gradual rebuilding of a new agriculture and new rural life." In
addition to implying that most country people were neither intelligent nor progressive, and that they needed government
aid and leadership, the commission more correctly recognized
that the most serious farm problem had persisted since the late
nineteenth century: farmers stood "practically alone against
organized interests." Industry, financiers, and transportation
companies had treated them unfairly, even discriminated
against them largely because farm men and women "lacked a
highly organized rural society."

Certainly farmers lacked the political power of their numbers. They had failed to unify and organize because of conflicting economic interests, geographic dispersion, and their
independent nature. The Country Life Commission recommended the organization of farmers to preserve their self-
interests. Specifically these were the improvement of rural
schools (especially through consolidation and curriculum reform), the building of all-weather highways to aid marketing
and reduce isolation, parcel post delivery, and agricultural
credit at low interest rates. The commission also recommended an extension service through the land-grant colleges,
which would apply agricultural research to daily farm needs;
crop diversification; the establishment of cooperatives; and
government regulation of monopolies. Many of these suggestions recalled the programs of the Grange, the Farmers' Alliance, and the People's party of the late nineteenth century.

Theodore Roosevelt agreed with the report. It was true, he
said, that country life "has improved greatly in attractiveness,
health and comfort, and that the farmer's earnings are higher
than they ever were. But city life is advancing even more rapidly." Most farm men and women, however, paid little atten-

tion to Roosevelt or the Country Life Commission, in part because they disliked being criticized by self-styled experts and
urban outsiders. They did, however, find champions in a
group of Democratic and Republican governors and members
of Congress from the major farm states who, in the reform
spirit of the age, became known as "progressives." Although
the term is less than precise because progressives comprised
ever-changing factions and interest groups, these reformers
sought various forms of social, political, and economic change.
During the early twentieth century many progressives from
the farm states, particularly in the Midwest, joined with their
urban colleagues to create the foundations of the activist, regulatory state in American agriculture. In the words of the
Country Life Commission, they believed that "government
should understand."

AGRICULTURAL ORGANIZATIONS

In the early years of the twentieth century, many
farmers advocated economic reform, but they differed widely
in their programs. While many wanted government regulation of economic activity to prevent abusive business practices,
farmers often disagreed about the specific methods of that
regulation. Congressional delegations in the farm states received sufficient encouragement from their constituents to advocate a variety of legislative changes that benefited farm men
and women but that also increased the regulatory power of the
federal government in ways that affected farm life, particularly in transportation, credit, and marketing.

Farm men and women now joined agricultural and commodity interest groups that dealt with specific farm problems
rather than advocating the kind of broad economic, political,
and social change that had characterized nineteenth-century
advocates. In part this change in approach stemmed from the

relatively good economic conditions that farmers were experiencing. They wanted to maintain and enhance their prosperity, but to do so they needed to adjust to changing business conditions. In 1904, for example, Iowa stockmen formed the Corn Belt Meat Producers Association for the purpose of dealing with railroad transportation problems in the Midwest.

Agricultural cooperatives emphasizing specific commodities such as wheat, corn, or cotton, in the form of grain elevators, livestock shipping associations, and cotton warehouses, became the most common type of farm organization, particularly in California, Minnesota, Wisconsin, Illinois, Iowa, New York, and the South. Cooperative members each cast one vote, and profits earned from the buying and selling of commodities and goods were returned to the members as dividends in proportion to the amount of business that the member conducted with the cooperative during the year. Cooperatives that emphasized the marketing of commodities were more profitable than those that also invested funds in the wholesale purchase of household and farm supplies for sale to its members, because members were not reliable patrons of their own cooperative stores.

In 1900 approximately 2,000 cooperatives served farmers nationwide, particularly in the dairying, wheat-, and corn-producing areas of the Midwest. The Minnesota Cooperative Creameries Association was a typical farm organization during the early twentieth century. Organized in 1911, it sold the butter and milk of more than 130 member cooperatives and operated a commission house in New York City. By 1920 approximately 1,000 livestock shipping associations served stockmen while almost 4,000 cooperatives received and sold grain. These cooperatives were designed to eliminate the middleman as well as establish farmer-owned stockyards and grain elevators at major and terminal markets. In 1912 agricultural cooperatives succeeded in encouraging the USDA to establish a cooperative fact-finding agency, called the Bureau of Markets, to provide the information needed for good marketing and purchasing decisions and thereby help increase farm profits.

Some farm cooperatives attempted to do more than eliminate the middleman and increase profits; they also sought to influence prices by controlling production or fixing prices. This voluntary activity usually failed, but the California Fruit Growers Exchange, organized in 1905 and later renamed Sunkist, gained greater marketing and pricing control by requiring its members to sell their fruit through the exchange or pay a fine. The exchange thus gained some control over marketing and bargained with distributors and processors for higher prices. This approach worked well where farmers produced specific commodities in a limited geographical area, because its members were less diffuse and the organization more disciplined in its actions. Commodity groups and farmers' cooperatives served as the chief instruments of political power for the more successful commercial farmers during the early twentieth century.

By 1920 the American Society of Equity and the Farmers' Union had become the two major farm organizations. The cooperative movement influenced both organizations, which in turn built on those activities. Founded in December 1902 in Indianapolis, the American Society of Equity drew its membership chiefly from among wheat farmers in Wisconsin, Minnesota, and the Dakotas. The Equity organized voluntary "holding campaigns" and urged farmers to refrain from marketing their commodities unless they received a price that the organization considered fair. It also established the Equity Cooperative Exchange to market wheat at the terminal market in Minneapolis. In Wisconsin the Equity became a strong supporter of Robert M. La Follette, the liberal wing of the Republican party, and the many economic and political reforms that helped characterize the Progressive Era. The Equity did not appeal to cotton farmers; they looked to the Southern Cotton Association or the Farmers' Union for support. And even in the areas of its strength, loose organization plagued the Equity. Many of its members soon forsook the organization for the Farmers' Union, but not before the Equity had established numerous grain and livestock shipping associations and helped educate farmers about the systematic marketing of commodities.

In 1902 the Farmers' Educational and Cooperative Union of America, known as the Farmers' Union (FU), had been organized in Texas under the leadership of Isaac Newton Gresham, a former member of the Farmers' Alliance. Soon it spread across the South and Midwest. In 1905 the FU became a national organization with membership restricted to farmers, agricultural workers, and the professional classes who served them, such as rural schoolteachers, ministers, doctors, and editors. Many of the organizers and leaders of the FU had been active in the Farmers' Alliance and the People's party, but they now advocated a more cautious, interest-group politics rather than a broad movement or political party. The Farmers' Union championed cooperative buying and selling through grain elevators, cotton warehouses, livestock shipping associations, and consumer stores. It also advocated cutting production and withholding crops (particularly cotton) from market to gain higher prices, and pledged to help farmers in marketing and in obtaining better prices for their products. The FU also wanted cheaper credit and more lending institutions. But it excluded black farmers, who organized their own cooperative, and it denied membership to bankers, merchants, lawyers, and speculators—those whom farmers believed had systematically cheated them in the past.

The Farmers' Union advocated economic reforms while avoiding party politics. The FU urged direct government intervention in the agricultural economy through regulatory legislation, particularly to guarantee cost-of-production prices for its commodities and a reasonable profit. It hoped to enlist a membership in the South and Midwest large enough to enable it to control the agricultural marketing of cotton and grain, and to gain favorable commodity prices through collective bargaining practices similar to those of organized labor. By 1920 other FU reform interests included railroad and banking regulation, lower tariffs, government-supplied credit, agricultural education in the public schools, and the outlawing of commodity speculation. All these goals were intended in part to expand the FU's appeal to farmers beyond the Midwest and South. The organization also advocated the eight-hour day and the end of convict and child labor in order to gain support from the working class. In general, though, the Farmers' Union wanted government aid to ensure farm profits, so long as it did not deny farmers freedom of action.

The Farmers' Union was unusual in linking wheat and cotton farmers in common cause for a number of economic reforms. Nationally, however, farm men and women had vastly different needs and interests. The South and West, for example, disagreed over high tariffs, depending on their interest in the export trade. Moreover, sharecroppers and tenant farmers had already proved during the Alliance years that they could not afford to participate in cooperative organizations. Fruit and vegetable growers in California and dairy farmers in the East also had few reasons to join the FU. In the Midwest, the Patrons of Husbandry, known as the Grange, emerged again as an organization that favored federal legislation to improve roads, deliver parcels, provide for the direct election of U.S. senators (in order to remove railroad influence from their selection in the statehouses), impose a national income tax (to lessen the burden on property taxes), and offer agricultural education and extension services. The Grange competed with the FU for members, based on these goals.

With the major agricultural organizations unable to unite farmers across the nation in common cause, or to achieve economic reform through joint political action, the Non-Partisan League (NPL) emerged as the most radical organization intent on solving the "farm problem." Organized in 1915 by Arthur C. Townley in North Dakota, the Non-Partisan League had little influence beyond state and regional politics. But through the NPL, farmers advocated economic reform through moderately socialist action. They sought to establish state-owned terminal grain elevators to provide proper grading and pricing of grain as well as to create state-owned banks, flour mills, and meatpacking plants, all through the support of politicians who advocated NPL goals.

The NPL skillfully used the direct primary system to support candidates in either major party for state offices. In 1917 the NPL-controlled legislature in North Dakota enacted legislation providing for a grain-grading system, guaranteed bank deposits, and a nine-hour workday for women. It also reduced tax rates on farm machinery, prohibited rate discrimination by railroads, and gave women the vote. Although the NPL collapsed even in North Dakota soon after the end of World War I because the Republican party had charged it with disloyalty for opposing America's entry into the war, it succeeded in winning legislative approval for a state bank that provided low-interest loans to farmers, a state mill and elevator, and compulsory and more affordable hail insurance through the state government. The NPL's achievements proved that government could aid agriculture, especially if farmers could control it.

REFORMERS, FARMERS, AND THE REGULATORY STATE

Although the People's party died in 1896, the agrarian reform movement gained new life during the early twentieth century. In the Midwest and South, many farmers as small-scale capitalists continued to believe that only the power of the federal government could protect them from the unfair practices of monopolies. In the Midwest particularly, many farmers saw nothing wrong with a powerful government and regulatory state as long as they could control it. Indeed, by 1906 agrarian discontent enabled reform-minded politicians such as Midwestern governors Robert M. La Follette of Wisconsin, Albert B. Cummins of Iowa, and Coe Crawford of South Dakota, as well as Southern governors Jeff Davis of Arkansas, Benjamin R. Tillman of South Carolina, James K. Vardaman of Mississippi, and Hoke Smith of Georgia (the latter three soon to win Senate seats) to attack monopolistic railroad practices that discriminated against farmers and diminished their income. Along with farm-state and middle-class reformers in Congress, including senators George Norris of Nebraska, Joseph Bristow of Kansas, Jonathan Dolliver of Iowa, and Joseph W. Bailey of Texas, they would achieve many of the goals of the Country Life Commission.

Strong Midwestern and Southern support for railroad regulation enabled the federal government to set equitable rates and prohibit rebates and rate discrimination. It also permitted Republicans and Democrats as well as urban and rural coalitions to work on behalf of farmers as well as businessmen, who also had rate grievances with the railroads. In 1905 Theodore Roosevelt, never one to trail public opinion, declared that the time had come "to assert the sovereignty of the National government by affirmative action." Soon Congress approved the Hepburn Act (1906), which granted the Interstate Commerce

Commission (ICC) the power to set maximum reasonable railroad rates upon the complaint of a shipper, subject to court review of the commission's actions (including its determination of the rates). The ICC was also given the power to inspect the financial records of railroads and prescribe railroad bookkeeping practices. Republican Representative Jonathan Dolliver of Iowa and Democrat Senator Benjamin R. Tillman of South Carolina led the successful fight to achieve passage, but only after President Roosevelt brokered a compromise in the Senate. The Hepburn Act was a major development in the federal regulation of private industry because it enabled the ICC to set railroad rates—usually lower—which in turn benefited farmers.

In 1910 the Mann-Elkins Act further aided farmers by extending railroad regulation. It allowed the ICC to set railroad rates on its own initiative and required the railroads to prove that ICC-established rates were inequitable. By World War I progressive farm-state reformers had joined with their urban counterparts to bring the railroads to heel, using the power of the government to require competition, set rates, break up monopolies, and end favoritism for large-scale shippers. Although some reformers, such as William Jennings Bryan, continued to favor nationalization of the railroads, most farmers preferred federal regulation, not ownership. Progressive-era rhetoric notwithstanding, ending "favoritism" to big shippers and rate discrimination was in fact anti-competitive. Such practices had been the result of competition. At least some of these "reforms," because they were anti-competitive, were welcomed by the railroads.

Midwest reformers also began to oppose the protective tariff, except on the importation of Canadian agricultural products, and join forces with Southerners to lower it. The Dingley Tariff of 1897 had imposed the highest rates in American history, averaging a 52 percent tax on goods shipped into the country. Many farmers believed the tariff aided only Eastern manufacturers and bankers, who sold their goods at excessive prices and who charged high interest rates. In 1901 Governor Cummins advocated what became known as the "Iowa Idea." He proposed abolishing the tariff on all trust-made products, a proposal that won great popularity in the farm states.

In 1909 a group of Midwestern progressive Republican senators attacked the pending Payne-Aldrich tariff bill because they wanted substantially lower rates for industrial goods and protection for agricultural products such as grain and livestock, but they failed to defeat it. Two years later President William Howard Taft, partly to embarrass Midwestern progressives, whom he believed had become his political enemies, pushed the Canadian Reciprocity Treaty through the Senate. Although the treaty lowered import taxes on Canadian goods, it permitted the importation of Canadian grain and cattle duty free.

The tariff issue continued to divide farmers regionally. Southern farmers, who sold most of their cotton crop abroad, wanted a low tariff in order to reduce the prices of manufactured goods. A high tariff did not increase the price of cotton, but it did increase their living costs while inviting retaliation against American agricultural products by other nations. Grain and livestock farmers believed, essentially incorrectly, that tariff protection prevented other nations from selling their farm commodities cheaply on the U.S. market, even though American farmers produced those commodities in surplus and faced little importation of agricultural products.

As a result of differing interests, substantive tariff reform did not come about until 1913, when Democratic reformers in Congress, with strong support from President Woodrow Wilson, united to pass the Underwood Tariff. It reduced rates on manufactured goods to pre–Civil War levels, with agricultural machinery placed on the free list. Congress also approved a federal income tax to replace revenues lost to tariff reduction. In addition, the Clayton Anti-Trust Act of 1914, with strong support from the Farmers' Union and the Farmers' National Congress, exempted agricultural organizations such as cooperatives from prosecution for restraint of trade.

Farmers of both parties also advocated a large, government-subsidized rural banking system to free them from dependence on private moneylenders. In 1913 Congress passed the Federal Reserve Act, which created twelve regional banks under a government-controlled Federal Reserve Board. The Federal Reserve banks issued paper money, redeemable in gold, and the board had the power to oversee and veto the interest rates of regional Reserve banks. Congress intended the Federal Reserve to provide order and stability to a banking system that had often been volatile and chaotic. The Federal Reserve banks would lend money to other banks, which could then lend money to farmers. This was viewed as a particular benefit at harvest time, when agricultural prices were lowest because commodities flooded the market. Many farmers preferred to sell at a later date if they could borrow other funds for living expenses. Reformers intended the Federal Reserve in part to improve the money supply and credit system for farmers, especially in the South and West. Equally important, for the first time farmers could now borrow money by using land and commodities as security.

But farmers still needed low-interest, long-term credit to finance their operations, and businessmen supported credit for farm production because they would benefit from the sale of seed, equipment, and goods for daily living. President Woodrow Wilson sympathized with the farmers and contended that agricultural problems in large measure stemmed from inadequate credit institutions. Although the Federal Reserve Act improved banking facilities and provided a flexible currency supply, it did not improve agricultural credit. Wilson contended that "credit based on cattle is as good as credit based on bills of lading." By 1916 the demand for low-interest credit was "nearly universal in the agricultural regions." The Wilson administration supported the Federal Farm Loan bill to avoid alienating the farm vote in a presidential election year. When passed, the act created a network of twelve Federal Land Banks modeled after the Federal Reserve System. These banks operated with an initial investment of federal capital and loaned money to private banks, which in turn made loans to cooperative farm organizations and individuals and took land as security. Federal Land Banks offered long-term loans ranging from twenty to forty years with land and improvements as security at interest rates not to exceed 6 percent annually.

The credit contributions of the Federal Land Banks proved modest because they made only long-term loans for mortgages. They did not provide short-term loans for the purchase of seed and equipment, or to help cooperatives market crops in an orderly fashion. Renters and tenants could not borrow through the Federal Land Bank system because they did not own land that could be used as collateral to secure the loan. Nevertheless, through the Federal Farm Loan Act the farm-state reformers in Congress and their rural supporters had achieved an unprecedented injection of federal funds into farm regions that needed capital. The federal government had taken a major departure by becoming directly involved in the agricultural economy.

Reform-minded Democrats and Republicans from the South, Midwest, and West also passed the Rural Post Roads Act in 1916. In response to the Good Roads Movement to improve farm-to-market roads and mail service, as well as to mollify bicycling organizations, President Wilson declared that, in the spirit of the Country Life Commission, good roads would "promote a fuller and more attractive rural life." Pro-

gressive reformers in Congress also gained sufficient support
to pass the Cotton Futures Act (1914), which standardized
grading, restricted speculation and market manipulation, and
helped end fraudulent practices on the New York Cotton Exchange; and the Grain Standards Act (1916), which required
the grading of grain by inspectors under federal license to ensure standardization and fairness. The Warehouse Act (1916)
enabled farmers to store some commodities, such as cotton, in
USDA-regulated warehouses and use the receipt as collateral
for bank loans. This legislation also authorized the licensing of
commodity inspectors, graders, weighers, and bondsmen, and
it gave the USDA responsibility for their supervision, thereby
bringing greater federal support and regulation to agriculture.
Certainly this legislation helped modernize agricultural marketing and create a national farm marketing system, but it also
expanded the regulatory power of the USDA.

This spate of farm legislation had been pushed by the
Farmers' Union and other agricultural groups, but the Wilson
administration, with strong support from Southern congressmen, provided the leadership to achieve tariff, banking, credit,
transportation, and agricultural marketing reform, and the
initiation of a federal income tax. Although the Federal Reserve System failed to satisfy farmers who still demanded better banking and credit facilities, the Federal Farm Loan and
Warehouse acts met some of their needs.

Lots of legislation

THE STATE AND AGRICULTURAL EDUCATION

During the late nineteenth century the Patrons of
Husbandry, commonly known as the Grange, and the Farmers' Alliance demanded that the land-grant colleges provide
practical agricultural education rather than the classical studies that prevailed in many private and public colleges and
universities. The land-grant colleges attempted to gain the

how was farming knowledge transferred?

what type of education

political and financial support of farmers by responding with a battery of short courses held under the rubric of Farmers' Institutes. These were held both on and off campus and helped diffuse farmers' discontent. At one of these institutes, farmers met for several days and listened to experts tell them how to improve their farming practices, with each session focused on a specific subject, such as breeding dairy cows, fertilizing fields, or marketing crops. Farm women also participated in programs designed to improve their work in the home, particularly regarding matters of health, nutrition, and cooking. These women, however, proved even more intractable than their men in their reluctance to accept advice, particularly from a university-trained woman, and they were less supportive of the institutes. Nonetheless, by the turn of the twentieth century these "adult" farmers' schools had achieved great popularity before peaking around 1912.

The black land-grant colleges also began offering institutes for African-American farmers around 1900, and Tuskegee Institute in Alabama developed the most successful program. Tuskegee farmers' institutes supported the philosophy of Booker T. Washington, who advocated economic advancement based on practical education rather than social equality for African Americans. In 1903 Tuskegee offered educational programs to 1,000 black farmers, and a year later it held 139 meetings across Alabama.

By 1914 many agricultural experts were complaining that the institutes failed to attract young farm men and women while the older attendees were using the programs more as a social gathering rather than to learn new methods they could apply to their farms. One critic noted that older farmers "gathered around the stove and talked and swapped stories, waiting for someone to come and pour some information into them, which would run out, or rather off, as fast as it was poured on." More important, though, was the fact that lecturers at the farmers' institutes did not visit individual farms to make demonstrations. A search began for a more effective way to inform farmers about the practical discoveries at the land-grant colleges and experiment stations.

   In 1903 the USDA had begun to provide practical agricultural education through the use of demonstration farms in the South. Seaman A. Knapp, a farmer and professor of agriculture at Iowa State College, and a contributor to the 1887 Hatch Act which established the state experiment station system, directed a USDA program to create five demonstration farms in Louisiana and Texas modeled after similar work he had established among rice farmers along the Gulf Coast during the mid-1880s. Knapp believed that farmers would improve their agricultural practices if they could see the results of applied techniques instead of relying on lectures at the farmers' institutes or bulletins from the agricultural experiment stations. Knapp worked on the premise that "What a man hears, he may doubt. What he sees, he may possibly doubt. But what he does himself, he cannot doubt."

   Knapp met with farmers and businessmen and asked them to select a farmer who would be willing to try the techniques that USDA scientists believed would improve agriculture in their area. To encourage these farmers to let the USDA use their land as a "demonstration farm," Knapp solicited support from businessmen and bankers to guarantee against loss of income if the new techniques failed. The USDA would provide guidance in the form of technical and managerial expertise, which the farmer agreed to follow. Nearby farmers would observe the results and hopefully try them on their own farms, thereby gradually improving agricultural practices over a wide area.

   Knapp established the first demonstration farm in Terrell County, Texas, and the cooperating farmer earned $700 more from his crops that year than he had previously. Knapp used this success to gain congressional support for demonstration work to combat the boll weevil across the cotton South. He hired demonstration workers, called "county agents," to establish demonstration farms to fight the boll weevil and to improve Southern agriculture by promoting diversification, crop rotation, improved seeds, better livestock, and new cultivation techniques. These efforts became known as the Farmers' Cooperative Demonstration Work (FCDW), which in 1906 also began helping African-American farmers by establishing demonstration farms with the use of two black county agents and by working with black land-grant colleges in Alabama and Virginia. Knapp reported that large-scale cotton plantation owners "actually object to having diversification taught to the tenants because they fear the tenants will become independent and leave their employ." But white and black farmers, whether landowners, tenants, or sharecroppers, supported Knapp's efforts to improve the cotton crop and thereby their income. A small-scale farmer in Mississippi reported that farmers in his area watched a nearby demonstration farm "like a hawk watches a spring chicken." In Texas a black farmer observed, "If President Roosevelt thinks enough of us . . . to send a white man down here to tell us how to raise cotton, I think we ought to raise cotton."

By 1910 white and black county agents were working with farmers in every Southern state. Four years later Knapp had 859 demonstration agents in the fields (one-fourth of whom in 1914 were women) and more than 1,000 farmers participating in the demonstration program. With the success of the FCDW, farmers increasingly looked to the federal government for expertise and support to make them more profitable and improve their standard of living, and farm-state politicians gave the FCDW their support.

The land-grant colleges opposed the work of the FCDW because they believed it infringed on their prerogatives, responsibilities, and congressional appropriations. While the USDA often distrusted agricultural experts who were academic scientists, administrators at the land-grant colleges did not believe county agents were qualified to teach farmers through demonstrations about new scientific, technological, and management techniques. But the demonstration work of the FCDW proved so popular, especially in the South, that the land-grant colleges could not kill the program. So they began working to gain control of its administration, programming, and funding. They achieved this goal in 1914 with the passage of the Smith-Lever Agricultural Extension Act.

Before passage of the Smith-Lever Act, the USDA agreed that the nation should have a unified extension system. Secretary of Agriculture David F. Houston recognized that researchers at the land-grant colleges had the knowledge and the advantage of location to reach farm men and women in the most efficient manner. Houston believed that agricultural extension should be a cooperative undertaking between the federal government, represented by the USDA, and the states, represented by the land-grant colleges. College officials agreed to administer the program with federal and state matching funds.

In 1914, Asbury F. Lever, chairman of the House Committee on Agriculture, introduced a bill "to provide cooperative agricultural extension work between the agricultural colleges and the United States Department of Agriculture." By demonstration work, farm men and women could be taught to be more efficient and productive. Secretary Houston explained: "A farmer is rather prejudiced; he is conservative and rather hardheaded. He is a man of sense and wants to be shown, and he is skeptical until he is shown." Congress agreed, and President Wilson signed the Smith-Lever Act in May to "aid in diffusing among the people . . . useful and practical information on subjects relating to agriculture and home economics and to encourage the application of the same." This legislation provided federal funds, matched with state and county money, for hiring demonstration agents—male for farm, female for home—and it authorized the land-grant college in each state to administer the agricultural extension program.

Specifically this legislation enabled the land-grant colleges to establish a cooperative extension service staffed by agents. They would circulate among farmers in their assigned territory to demonstrate new techniques and disseminate information that would help farm men and women improve their productivity, efficiency, and quality of life. In this way the research of the USDA, experiment stations, and the land-grant colleges would become available to farm men and women. Congress required the states to match federal funding for the initial $10,000 authorized to each state annually, plus additional federal funds based on rural population figures.

Rural congressmen gave the Smith-Lever Act strong support, but some urban representatives charged that it permitted federal intrusion in local affairs and that it would lead to socialism. Senator James Vardaman of Mississippi responded that "The highest end of government is the improvement of Man." Vardaman and many other farm-state congressmen believed the federal government had a responsibility to aid the farm community through research and education. By 1917 some fourteen hundred extension agents circulated among farmers and demonstrated new farming practices and shared information from the agricultural scientists working in the USDA (which by the turn of the twentieth century had become one of the most important research institutions in the world) and at the experiment stations and land-grant colleges.

Farmers also sought federal support for "practical" agricultural instruction in the public schools. The Grange and other farm organizations strongly advocated federal aid and leadership to promote agricultural training in the high schools. In February 1917 Congress responded by passing the Smith-Hughes Act, which authorized federal aid to schools that provided vocational, agricultural, and home economics education. Farmers thus placed greater reliance on the federal government to do what they lacked the resources and expertise to accomplish for themselves. The growing involvement of the federal government in agriculture also became apparent in increased congressional appropriations for the USDA, which jumped from $2.8 million in 1899 to $28 million by 1917. President Wilson believed this support strengthened the nation's "great agricultural foundations."

central
power

THE USDA AND THE EXPANSION OF FEDERAL POWER

The USDA, especially, had benefited from the emergence of the regulatory state. Much of the groundbreaking legislation concerning agriculture created new responsibilities for the agency, including forest conservation (1905), pure food and drugs (1906), meat inspection (1906), and export and certification duties (1908). By the end of World War I the USDA ranked second only to the Treasury Department in numbers of employees. These employees had broad responsibilities for planning and the application of agricultural expertise to farm problems, and they showed contempt for the radical solutions that had been offered by the rural reformers of the late nineteenth century.

Essentially the new farm legislation authorized the USDA to collect information, conduct investigations, and compel compliance. Certainly many of the laws expanded the role of the USDA as a service institution to support the modernization of agriculture. It became more than the information-gathering and -disseminating agency of the late nineteenth century. During the first two decades of the twentieth century the USDA became a bureaucratic regulatory agency with considerable powers to represent the federal government.

Populist demands for regulation, nationalization, and monetary and tax reform had proven that many farmers were not opposed to the expansion of state power. Indeed, they welcomed it to protect the general welfare. During the early twentieth century, however, many farmers also became amenable to—even if ambivalent about—the creation of a distant bureaucracy of experts who increasingly dictated farmer actions through legislation and programs designed for their own good. Urban reform-minded congressmen saw little threat from farm-state reformers because they too championed the benefits of a regulatory state, administered by a bureaucracy of experts who served those who lived in the city as well as in the countryside. At the same time many of the new federal regulatory activities in agriculture came in part from the advocacy of farmers themselves; they were not always top-down mandates of the USDA. The USDA also used the principle of local administration—that is, participatory regulation and cooperative administration with farmers at the county and state levels—to gain support for the expansion of regulatory and administrative powers.

In the Progressive Era, then, farmers and their congressional representatives achieved many of the goals that had been advocated by reformers during the late nineteenth century. Although the composition of farm leadership had changed, and while coalitions formed and dissolved as issues were won and lost, and while the urban middle-class base of the progressive movement cannot be denied, farmers helped bring many features of industrialism and capitalism under regulation and control. By so doing, these reform-minded farmers played an important role in the formation of the regulatory state.

WORLD WAR I   *who set prices?*

World War I brought profits for the American
farmer. Agricultural prices rose soon after the conflict broke
out in early August 1914 and rose still higher when the United
States entered the war in April 1917. British farmers could not
meet that country's military and civilian needs; the war prevented the importation of Russian wheat through normal
channels; and farmers in northern France were drafted or had
their lands overrun. American farmers soon provided much of
the food and fiber needed to support Britain and France,
which Woodrow Wilson chose to call "Associated Powers"
once the United States joined the conflict. Although farmers
quickly profit from war (unless they are killed or have their
homes and lands destroyed) because agricultural prices are
among the first to rise, war also demands state planning and
the regulation of public life, including agriculture. World War
I increased the regulatory involvement of the federal government in farm life and furthered the statist relationship between the federal government and the American farmer.

In 1917, for example, Congress passed the Food Production
Act, which authorized the USDA to place farm and home
demonstration agents in every agricultural county in the nation, even if those counties did not want the imposed bureaucracy or mandated shared expense of supporting them. These
county agents helped locate and allocate seed, fertilizer, equipment, and credit for farmers, and recruited agricultural workers. The county agents also sat on draft boards and helped
determine which young men would receive deferments to remain on the farm and contribute to the war effort through
agricultural production. Congress also passed the Food Control Act or Lever Act (1917), which gave President Wilson dic-
tatorial control over the distribution and consumption of food

through the newly created U.S. Food Administration headed by Herbert Hoover. Under the Food Control Act, Wilson set the minimum price of wheat for 1917 at $2.20 per bushel, later raised to $2.26 per bushel for the 1918 crop, to encourage maximum production. Farmers responded by producing 921 million bushels of wheat, of which 287 million were shipped abroad. As a result of wartime demands and accompanying inflation, farm income increased from approximately $7.5 billion annually for the period 1909–1914 to about $17.7 billion in 1919.

Adopting the motto "Food Will Win the War," the Food Administration asked farmers to increase production to meet domestic and foreign needs, particularly in wheat. In the decade before 1914, farmers had planted approximately 48 million acres of wheat annually. Rapid price increases and government urging boosted the total to 60 million acres, which in 1915 produced a record crop of more than 1 billion bushels. By May 1917 wheat reached $3.48 per bushel on some markets, although speculators on the Chicago Futures Market rather than farmers reaped most of the benefits of escalating prices.

In order to ensure an adequate supply of pork the Food Administration also worked with buyers to guarantee a price of $15.50 per hundredweight for hogs, when approximately $9.75 per hundredweight would have guaranteed a profit. The Chicago Board of Trade established a relatively low price of $1.28 per bushel of corn to encourage farmers to feed it to hogs and market it as pork. As a result, hog prices increased to over $17.50 per hundredweight in 1918 and to more than $19 per hundredweight in 1919. Beef exports, meanwhile, rose from 150 million pounds in 1914 to 954 million pounds four years later. Although the Food Administration did not guarantee a price for beef, demand increased beef prices from $6.24 per hundredweight in 1914 to $9.56 per hundredweight in 1919.

By the time of the Armistice in 1918, livestock raisers had increased cattle numbers by 20 percent nationwide. Similarly the price of dairy products increased 70 percent by the end of the war. Cotton prices also rose from about 8 cents per pound in 1914 to 38 cents per pound in 1919.

The Food Administration attempted to keep consumer prices from rising to unacceptable inflationary levels. It also encouraged consumers to limit consumption by observing wheatless Mondays and Wednesdays and meatless Tuesdays, and to conserve foods such as sugar by substituting honey and sorghum. The Food Administration also licensed food processors and retailers in order to prevent waste and hoarding and to control production and pricing, under penalty of closing those businesses for noncompliance. Farmers complained about this federal intervention because they considered prices too low, but the government kept agricultural prices high enough to ensure considerable profit without creating a hardship for consumers.

In fact farmers had never earned such high prices as during World War I. Although they had advocated a regulatory state in order to improve their lives, they now considered the federal government intrusive when it set prices and refused to allow them to rise to maximum levels. But this attitude prevailed when prices were high and production full. When the war ended and agricultural prices collapsed, farmers quickly advocated government intervention to set prices in their favor, thus supporting dependency in time of need. Many farmers no doubt agreed with Arthur C. Townley, leader of the Non-Partisan League, who said that if the federal government could keep prices down in time of war, it could surely keep them up in time of peace. Indeed, the most important effects of World War I were the regulatory entanglement of the federal government in agriculture and the realization by farmers that if government policy could alter economic conditions for them during war, it could aid them during a time of economic emergency.

In sum, after 1912 the Wilson administration, with support from farm-state congressmen, particularly from the South, achieved more legislation designed to aid farmers than ever before. Farmers increasingly looked to federal help in solving their economic problems, which in turn fostered their dependence on the federal government for assistance in the form of tariff reduction, railroad regulation, and banking and credit programs. By pushing through legislation that lowered the tariff, established an income tax, strengthened railroad regulation, inaugurated a new banking system, improved anti-trust legislation, regulated commodity trading, expanded the agricultural extension system, and permitted the executive branch to determine agricultural prices, Congress and farmers clearly moved away from the Jeffersonian ideal that championed minimal government and maximum personal independence. During the first two decades of the twentieth century, farmers demanded a fundamental and major expansion of government aid, which involved greater regulation of agriculture. This groundswell of reform legislation improved agrarian life economically, socially, and educationally. At the same time farmers played an important role in the creation of a new "statist" relationship with the federal government.

The roots of this newly emerging statism lay in the agrarian revolt of the late nineteenth century—in the anti-monopoly parties of the 1870s, the Greenback movement of the 1880s, and the Farmers' Alliance and People's party of the late 1880s and 1890s. The activities of the last thirty years of the nineteenth century provided the foundation for the broad expansion, if not the creation, of the regulatory state. Although most farmers nationwide hated bureaucracy because of its expense and its propensity to deny freedom of action, they recognized

the need for an expanded bureaucracy to manage the regulatory legislation they considered essential for the improvement
of agricultural life.

During the first two decades of the twentieth century, farmers began to create a "producer-friendly" state, the likes of
which they had advocated since the 1870s. Their goal was to
expand the economic and regulatory power of the nation to
help ensure an equitable distribution of wealth in American
society. Farmers and farm-state politicians provided important leadership for the agriculturally related reforms of the
Progressive Era because they had many long-standing grievances, and they were committed to seeking change through
the political process, usually within the two-party system.
They also wanted the federal government to exercise a variety
of economic and regulatory powers for the benefit of farmers
as a class. Farmers saw no danger or inequity in class legislation as long as it benefited them.

Despite regional, class, ethnic, and racial differences, farmers had sufficient unity and collective purpose to achieve
substantive political change. They used the expanded administrative powers of the federal government to create a new regulatory state largely because their problems were national and
could not be solved at local, county, or state levels. Farmers in
the South, Midwest, and West dominated the politics of their
regions, of course, but they also formed coalitions with urban-
rural areas, particularly in the Midwest where voters reviled
monopoly and abusive corporate power.

Thus farm men and women turned increasingly to national
legislation, and agricultural issues became matters of public
policy during the first two decades of the twentieth century.
While few would argue that the agricultural reform legislation of the Progressive Era harmed farmers, much of it also
made them increasingly dependent on the federal government
for the improvement of their lives.

2

The Age of Uncertainty

BY 1920 American farm men and women had developed the most productive, diverse, and profitable agriculture in the world. Nearly 32 million people, including 925,000 African Americans, occupied 6.4 million farms, which averaged about 149 acres. In the South, sharecroppers and tenants remained the smallest-scale farmers with about 50 acres each. At least half the white farmers were tenants, while tenancy and sharecropping rates combined for black farmers reached as high as 90 percent in some areas. Across the South, poverty remained the prevailing agricultural condition. Few Southern farmers owned telephones, trucks, or tractors, or lighted their homes with electricity. The collapse of high wartime prices exacerbated the economic problems of Southern tenant farmers and sharecroppers because their operating costs remained high. Credit, cultivated acreage, transportation, markets, capital, and mechanization remained inadequate. Most Southern farmers lived in desperation and without alternatives to improve their economic fate. They were locked in perpetual poverty.

Across the country soil, climate, and markets determined regional differences between farmers. In the North, dairy farming remained important in New England, where by 1920 the Boston milk shed reached into southern Maine and north-

eastern New York. Branch railroads and trucks enabled farmers to ship milk to distant markets relatively easily, if not
always cheaply. Milk dealers now assumed the tasks of distribution and sales. By 1930 most farmers in New Hampshire,
Vermont, and Maine depended on the monthly milk check for
their primary income. In the Midwest, farmers continued to
raise corn, which they used to fatten hogs and cattle, but they
also produced large quantities of milk in Wisconsin, Minnesota, and Michigan. Farmers in the Midwest cornbelt produced most of the high-protein foods—meat and dairy
products—for family tables cross the nation, while farmers in
the Great Plains emphasized wheat and cattle, and in the
Southern plains, cotton. In the Far West, large-scale farmers
in California continued to raise vegetables and fruits and increasingly cotton, as did farmers in Arizona.

Overall by 1920 the cash grain and livestock farmers in the
Midwest, dairy farmers in New England, truck farmers in the
Middle Atlantic states, and large-scale farmers who produced
fruits and vegetables as well as wheat and cattle in the Far
West enjoyed economic prosperity. African-American and
white tenants and sharecroppers in the South, however, often
cultivated fewer than fifty acres and earned less than $200 a
year under the crop lien system. Bound to their landlords in
continuing contracts, they lived little above slavery.

Postwar Decline

Before 1920 the agricultural economy had been
strong. Farmers took advantage of high wartime commodity
prices to purchase more land, buy new machinery, and improve their buildings. Seldom, however, did they pay for these
purchases and improvements with cash. They bought on
credit or took mortgages on their new acquisitions. As long as
prices remained high, they were able to meet their repayment
obligations.

The absence of credit had always been a major problem for farmers because their income was irregular and uncertain. Farmers needed credit at low interest rates over many months to cover operating and daily living expenses. Banks relied on deposits for their loan funds, but depositors could withdraw their money on demand. Consequently banks set loan rates relatively high, around 7 percent, and the loan period short, ranging from three to six or nine to twelve months. Livestock producers particularly needed longer repayment periods of one to three years in order to raise, feed, and market cattle at a profitable weight. Given the customarily short loan periods, however, farmers usually had to repay the loan before they sold the crops or livestock that the loan had enabled them to plant, purchase, and raise. Moreover, lower agricultural prices meant less farm income and shrinking bank deposits, which also brought a decline in loanable funds. Although the Federal Farm Loan Act of 1916 improved the long-term loan rate for real estate mortgages, farmers still needed cheap, long-term operating loans. And if banks failed, farmers had to pay their loans or find other ways to refinance them, sometimes losing their deposits as well.

Remarkably, most farmers ignored the possibility of a severe adjustment of the agricultural economy with the end of the war. But in the summer of 1920, agricultural prices dropped sharply. The price of corn declined by 78 percent, wheat fell 64 percent, and cotton dropped 57 percent. Livestock prices fell 32 percent, then dropped again by December 1921 from a postwar high of $16.45 to $7.31 per hundredweight for beef. Economists estimated that corn production costs now exceeded the selling price by 50 percent. Similarly the price for burley tobacco fell from 33 cents to 13 cents per pound while bright Southern tobacco declined from 44 cents to 21 cents per pound. A 5-million-bale carryover of the cotton crop also dropped prices from 41 to 10 cents per pound by June 1921, below the prewar average. Cotton farmers responded by

planting still more acreage and demanding special credit help
from the federal government. Similarly the wheat surplus remained high, and prices declined accordingly from $2.96 per
bushel in July to 92 cents per bushel in December. As net farm
income fell from $9 billion in 1919 to $3.3 billion in 1921—
which translated into a drop from $1,395 to $517 per farm—
and as land values plummeted, farm bankruptcies grew. Many
farmers who had invested in land and equipment when agricultural prices were high now found they could not meet their
obligations.

Farmers owed commercial, savings, and federal land banks,
mortgage and insurance companies, and other lenders, often
at interest rates as high as 12 percent. Small-scale, inefficient
farmers who had not committed to one-crop commercial agriculture lived in fear of foreclosure or poverty, because their
purchasing power declined faster than their operating expenses, based on the parity price index for the period from
1909 to 1914. Once the recession ended, farm prices averaged
about 30 percent more than during the prewar years. But the
wartime debts that farmers had accumulated at wartime
prices proved difficult to repay.

By 1921 American agricultural production exceeded domestic and international demand. As farm prices fell, nonfarm
prices declined more slowly, and farm men and women became caught in a cost-price squeeze—they earned less for their
labor but still paid high prices for everything they purchased.
A year after the agricultural recession began, farmers found
themselves with only two-thirds of the purchasing power they
had enjoyed in 1913. Some farmers responded to their situation by planting more acres and raising more livestock to
make up in volume for the decline in prices. Other farmers reduced production because low earnings prevented them from
purchasing more seed, fertilizer, and implements, including
tractors. They also tried to become more efficient by cutting

costs or delaying the purchase of new equipment, but these attempts often prevented them from achieving their goal. For example, in delaying the purchases of new machinery they found it difficult to reduce labor costs and increase production. By the late 1920s, farm foreclosures increased from fewer than 4 per 1,000 before World War I to 17 per 1,000.

The agricultural recession that began in 1920 lasted three years. In many respects it was simply an economic correction to the rapid expansion of production that had been stimulated by the war. By 1920 European farmers, particularly French and British, once again began to meet many of the food needs of their people. At the same time European governments had little money for the purchase of American agricultural commodities, and by 1922 U.S. farm exports declined from $3.8 billion to $1.9 billion. Canadian, Argentinean, and Australian farmers sold greater quantities of wheat and beef on the international market, reducing American sales as well as lowering the world price for these commodities. American farmers also raised exceptionally large crops of wheat, corn, rice, and tobacco, and these surpluses further depressed commodity prices.

Although agricultural prices did not fall below prewar levels, a half-million farmers suffered bankruptcy largely because they had overinvested in land and equipment during the war years. Throughout the 1920s the situation remained grim for many more. Most farmers had come to expect an improved standard of living based on high wartime prices. Automobiles and telephones had become necessities for many farmers, and they did not wish to forgo the luxury of disposable income. By 1925, though farmers received an index price of 95 compared to an average index price of 72 for the period between 1910 and 1914, wheat and cotton farmers became especially vocal in demanding that government do something to improve agricultural prices and the farm economy.

after only 3 years?

By 1929 farm men and women had increased production by
13 percent over 1917 and provided about $2 billion in agricul-
tural commodities for export—35 percent of the nation's export trade. This increase in production was largely due to the
use of more fertilizer, improved seed, new technology, and
better methods. Still, agricultural prices lagged behind production costs. By 1930 farmers paid an index price of 151 for
all purchases and earned an index price of 125 for their commodities; their "parity" purchasing power compared to
1909–1914 fell to 83.

Low prices, declining profits, and limited purchasing
power in return for seemingly unending work drove men and
women from farms into towns and cities, seeking better job
and earning opportunities. By 1930 the farm population had
fallen to 30.5 million, or about 25 percent of the population,
after peaking in 1916 at 32.5 million, or 32 percent of the population. The number of farms declined to 6.2 million, down
from 6.5 million in 1919. As the farm population fell, farm size
increased to an average 157 acres.

Overall by 1933 too many farmers still occupied the land
and tried to eke out a living without sufficient capital, equipment, or the ability to operate productively and efficiently.
Lower earnings, a heavy burden of debt, and shrinking markets prevented many farmers from enjoying a standard of living comparable to city dwellers. A high tariff made it difficult
for foreign nations to sell products to the United States and
buy agricultural commodities. Those who stayed on the land
increasingly demanded parity between the prices they received
for their commodities and the prices they paid for consumer
goods and farm necessities.

The postwar agricultural recession brought a fresh outburst
of complaints from farmers about their lack of control over
marketing and prices. When they sold their commodities they
could accept the price offered at the grain elevator, cotton

warehouse, or stockyards, or they could go back home. Until they were able to control production and marketing, they could not affect prices. In 1922 Secretary of Agriculture Henry C. Wallace advised, "It will never be possible for the farmers to relate their production to profitable demand with the nicety of the manufacturer, both because they cannot control the elements which influence production, and cannot estimate demand as closely." Farmers sold their commodities for wholesale prices but bought everything at retail prices. They understood that large corporations and manufacturers controlled prices by regulating production. But most farmers—with the exception of California fruit growers—could not organize collectively to control production and regulate prices because of regional and personal differences. Instead many farmers increasingly sought help from the federal government to intervene in the agricultural economy on their behalf, though they could not agree about the specific form of government aid. They also contended that they continued to need better credit—long-term loans with low interest rates.

Farmers now intensified their discussions about the proper role of government in the agricultural economy. Some contended that the federal government should confine itself to its historic role—providing information through the extension service, experiment stations, and land-grant colleges, to help farmers become more productive, efficient, and profitable, while regulating transportation and credit systems. Others advocated direct federal intervention in the farm economy to raise prices above the level set by supply and demand. Some suggested that the federal government make direct payments to farmers for reducing production. The Farmers' Union continued to demand that the government guarantee cost-of-production prices plus a reasonable profit. Still others proposed loaning money to foreign nations with the requirement that they use it to purchase American farm commodities.

Some farmers urged higher tariffs on foreign commodities and more emphasis on cooperative marketing, and others wanted the federal government to purchase the annual surplus of various crops at a profitable price for farmers, sell it abroad, and absorb any losses. Although farmers, agricultural experts, and policymakers could not agree on a plan to end the agricultural recession, they agreed that the nation had a farm problem—one they would continue to discuss for the remainder of the century. In all of these debates, farmers and their supporters referred to "parity" prices, that is, prices that gave farm men and women the same purchasing power they had enjoyed from 1909 to 1914.

The administration of Warren G. Harding believed that the decline in agriculture was just a self-correcting dip in the market economy and that recovery would soon follow, just as it had in earlier recessions. Farmers, however, had little patience for the natural flow of economic events. They wanted action from the federal government. In the words of the president of the Kansas Farmers' Union, they could "see no other way to help the farmer of this country, in this emergency, but by the action of the Government, and that immediately."

SCIENCE AND TECHNOLOGY

Those farmers in the 1920s who hoped to improve their profitability through new technology turned especially to gasoline-powered tractors, which symbolized mechanized farming. Steam engines had proved too large, cumbersome, and expensive for the average farm, but small gasoline tractors could be purchased for about $1,000 on credit. By eliminating feed crops, farmers gained about five acres for cash crops for every horse replaced by a tractor, usually two and often three or four horses per farm.

In 1924 the International Harvester Company revolutionized tractor technology by introducing the Farmall, which soon made the Fordson obsolete. The Farmall was the first low-priced, tricycle-design tractor built for row-crop farming, because it was built to travel down crop rows without damaging the plants. The Farmall was ideal for light work on truck and dairy farms and for cultivating corn. By 1925 small tractors like the Farmall were in wide use on dairy, vegetable, and fruit farms from New York to the Pacific Coast.

In the 1920s tractor manufacturers added a power take-off mechanism so that the engine could power other equipment such as combines and mowing machines. Pneumatic rubber tires also enabled tractors to travel on paved roads. As a result, the number of tractors on farms increased from 246,000 in 1920 to 920,000 in 1930, enabling grain farmers particularly to increase production, a factor that did not help farm prices. In 1920 U.S. Department of Agriculture (USDA) officials estimated that a farmer needed at least 130 acres to make the purchase of a tractor affordable. Many farmers who had overextended their finances during the war years found themselves unable to afford tractors that would make them more efficient and reduce labor costs.

Farmers in the Great Plains and the Far West, where large wheat fields prevailed in the 1920s, continued to purchase combines while the mechanical corn-picker brought revolutionary change to the Midwest, chiefly by cutting labor expenses. Even so, in this decade the gasoline-powered tractor became the most important technological development in American agriculture. Tractors provided efficient and dependable power and did not require rest periods as horses or mules did. Tractors also helped farmers do their necessary work, such as plowing, mowing hay, and harvesting, in the absence of adequate workers. Farmers who could afford tractors purchased more land because they could cultivate it efficiently as well as increase productivity. The increase in average farm acreage between 1920 and 1930 is partly attributable to tractor technology.

Tractor manufacturers urged farmers to adopt the new technology. In 1929 International Harvester warned farmers that "the man who places his dependence on muscle power is sadly handicapped." Yet gasoline tractors did not regain independence for farmers. They were increasingly tied to national and international affairs beyond their control, particularly regarding the purchase of oil and gasoline and repair parts. As they gave up their horses, they also had to rely more on outside suppliers for fertilizer. In order to afford these new purchases, farmers needed more income, which they often tried to achieve by purchasing more land and increasing productivity per acre. Thus farmers came to depend more on the land-grant colleges and state experiment stations as well as corporate research to provide the scientific and technological answers for their economic problems.

While mechanical engineers worked to build efficient, affordable tractors, agricultural scientists conducted research to improve seed varieties. They revolutionized crop production with the development of hybrid corn. This was seed produced by crossing two or more plants to produce a new plant with specific characteristics. Traditionally farmers and corn breeders had based the selection of seeds on the physical appearance of the kernels. They believed that seed corn had certain characteristics that could be identified by sight. At the turn of the twentieth century, however, several scientists began investigating the genetic characteristics of corn in relation to productivity, and they learned that specific characteristics could be isolated and controlled. Soon after World War I many scientists at state experiment stations and private seed companies in the Midwest developed hybrid corn breeding programs. In

1926 Henry A. Wallace, later secretary of agriculture and vice president under Franklin Delano Roosevelt, became the first commercial producer of hybrid corn.

At first farmers were reluctant to purchase hybrid corn for seed because it was more expensive and because they still believed the best seed could be selected simply by looking at it. Within a decade, however, they realized that hybrid corn increased yields per acre from 40 to 120 bushels. They could not, however, easily and efficiently produce hybrid corn seed for themselves; seeds from a hybrid ear degenerated on planting, and successive crops failed to produce crops similar to the first generation. Farmers thus had to depend on the seed companies each year for their hybrid corn crops.

Public and private science and technology, disseminated by county agents and corporate salesmen, offered farmers the opportunity to increase production to remain competitive in the marketplace. Yet the costs of scientific and technological efficiency also made it difficult for farmers to increase their earnings. In a sense, in the 1920s commercially oriented farmers climbed on the scientific and technological treadmill and then found they could not afford to get off. They could squeeze more productivity from the land, but they had to rely on federal and state research and education to do so, and no improvements were cheap.

AGRICULTURAL ORGANIZATIONS

Despite the decline in farm income, the agricultural economy never fell to a level that prompted political third-party solutions. The most ambitious attempt at a third party was Robert M. La Follette's bid for the presidency in 1924 as standard-bearer of the Progressive party. La Follette ran on a platform of his own making, attributing the economic hard times of grain farmers in the Midwest and West to government favoritism of corporations, excessive freight rates for farmers, and speculation in agricultural commodities. But he ran far behind President Calvin Coolidge on the Republican ticket and Democrat John W. Davis.

Unable to unite politically because of their differing economic needs, farmers sought solutions through cooperative marketing and interest-group politics. Many agricultural leaders and farmers believed that cooperatives would eliminate the charges of middlemen who bought and sold their commodities, and thereby make marketing more efficient and controllable. By 1925 approximately eleven thousand cooperatives did $2 billion in annual business and provided members with higher prices and better credit than they had had in acting alone. They chiefly sold grain, livestock, and milk. Most cooperatives, though, were too small to improve bargaining positions or prices substantially, or to enhance marketing efficiency. Only the largest and best-organized cooperatives, such as the California Fruit Growers Exchange, the Sun Maid Raisin Growers' Association, and the Land O'Lakes Creamery, achieved substantial market control.

Farmers and their supporters proved more effective through interest-group politics. The failure of the People's party convinced many farmers and agricultural leaders of the futility of third-party politics, while price controls during World War I proved the need for a farm voice in Congress. As a result, by 1920 the major farm organizations had established offices in Washington, D.C., to lobby for their members. The American Farm Bureau Federation, commonly known as the Farm Bureau, became the most important and influential farm organization to lobby Congress after it organized on a national basis in March 1920. With a membership of approximately 320,000 in 28 states and large coffers, the Farm Bureau effectively pressured Congress for aid.

The Farm Bureau developed from a group of state farm

bureaus. These were associations of commercially oriented and profitable farmers and businessmen who joined to support financially the work of county agents and extension services. From the beginning, the Farm Bureau considered farming a business like any other, and sought to make the business of farming more profitable by improving the "marketing, transportation, and distribution of farm products," particularly through cooperative marketing. Although the Farm Bureau opposed unnecessary government regulation of the economy, especially government-owned railroads and public utilities, it advocated greater federal support for the privately owned Federal Land Banks, tariff protection for farmers, and cooperative marketing. The Farm Bureau also wanted a federal farm policy that would benefit commercial agriculture.

In Washington the Farm Bureau monitored congressional voting and encouraged legislators to support issues of concern to the organization. Congressmen from the farm states came to consider support of the Farm Bureau a matter of political necessity, though it held little appeal for Southerners, who favored agricultural organizations that catered to cotton and tobacco farmers, such as the American Cotton Association (ACA) composed of growers, bankers, merchants, and warehousemen. The ACA worked to reduce cotton acreage and control marketing. But cotton farmers proved as unwilling as ever to maintain organizational discipline and sell their crop only through the ACA. Tobacco cooperatives experienced similar problems, though by the mid-1920s the Burley Tobacco Growers' Association achieved group solidarity and an estimated $143 million more in earnings for members than under the old system of individual sales. At the same time the Farmers' Union spread rapidly into the Great Plains where it appealed mainly to small-scale wheat farmers. It attacked the Farm Bureau as an agent of "big business," in part because the Farm Bureau worked closely with county agents and extension services to help farmers increase their productivity while the FU believed in withholding commodities from market and reducing production. The Farmers' Union accused the Farm Bureau of serving only large-scale, landowning, capital-intensive farmers.

In May 1921 a group of senators and representatives from the Great Plains, the Midwest, and the South informally created the Farm Bloc to improve agricultural conditions through nonpartisan legislation. The initial group consisted of Senators Kenyon of Iowa, Norris of Nebraska, Kendrick of Wyoming, Gooding of Idaho, Capper of Kansas, Smith of South Carolina, La Follette of Wisconsin, Sheppard of Texas, Ladd of North Dakota, Fletcher of Florida, Ransdell of Louisiana, and Heflin of Alabama. In the House the Farm Bloc organized under the leadership of Congressman Lester J. Dickinson of Iowa. Gray Silver, chief lobbyist for the Farm Bureau, addressed the initial meeting of this group and told the senators that farmers wanted the federal government to improve credit opportunities, protect cooperatives, regulate meatpacking companies and trading in grain futures, and improve farm-to-market roads. The members of the Farm Bloc worked with the Farm Bureau to address these agricultural issues.

Senator Arthur Capper of Kansas spoke for all members of the Farm Bloc when he declared that "national prosperity is dependent primarily upon agricultural prosperity," and that without prosperous farmers "the Nation cannot have a continued growth and development." Congressman Gilbert N. Haugen of Iowa agreed that without agricultural prosperity, "just as sure as the sun rises in the East and sets in the West . . . our factories and mills and our banks would crumble to pieces." In addition to voicing this Jeffersonian rhetoric, farm men and women and their congressional representatives believed that if the federal government could aid and protect industry, it could and should help farmers.

The Farm Bloc's legislative achievements strengthened federal administrative and regulatory power in agriculture. By late summer 1921 the Farm Bloc had gained passage of three important measures: the Packers and Stockyards Act, to prevent the manipulation of livestock prices by packers and speculators; the Emergency Agricultural Credits Act, authorizing the War Finance Corporation to make loans to banks and cooperative farm organizations to support the marketing of livestock in domestic and foreign trade; and an amendment to the Federal Farm Loan Act, to increase the capital of the Federal Land Banks and the minimum amount of loans. The Farm Bloc also supported the Highway Act of 1921, which provided funding for the construction of secondary highways, or farm-to-market roads. And in 1922 the Farm Bloc pushed through the Grain Futures Trading Act, which limited price fluctuations and provided greater regulation of the futures market.

The Farm Bloc also addressed farmers' desires for "orderly marketing," to prevent the flooding of markets at harvest time and the resulting lowering of prices. In February 1922 Congress responded with the Capper-Volstead Cooperative Marketing Act, which permitted agricultural cooperatives to pool resources and eliminate competition to improve marketing without violating the Clayton Anti-Trust Act. The Capper-Volstead Act also shifted enforcement of anti-trust restrictions for agricultural cooperatives from the Department of Justice to the friendlier USDA. The Farm Bloc also supported the Fordney-McCumber tariff, which placed heavy duties on more than two hundred agricultural commodities—ignoring the fact that the United States did not import staple crops already in surplus. The tariff in fact made American farm products more expensive for foreign buyers while increasing the cost of manufactured goods at home. Meanwhile the amended Grain Futures Act authorized congressional regulation of trading exchanges.

In March 1923 Congress also passed the Intermediate Agricultural Credits Act, designed to make the marketing of farm products a more orderly process. This legislation created twelve intermediate credit banks, under the supervision of the Federal Farm Loan Board, to loan funds to agricultural marketing associations. The federal government capitalized these new banks at $5 million each. The law also authorized the incorporation of private farm credit institutions to provide agricultural and livestock loans. The Intermediate Credits Act enabled farmers to borrow money through cooperatives to meet their financing needs between long-term and short-term loans. From the intermediate credit banks they could secure low-interest loans between planting time and the marketing of crops, usually about six months but sometimes as long as five years, to aid production as well as marketing. These loans would bridge the income gap during the year and enable farmers to meet basic expenses by using their crops and livestock as collateral.

This legislation, while important, proved insufficient to deal with the disparity between farm income and expenditures. Farmers began to demand "equality for agriculture," a federal plan to manage the supply and marketing of agricultural commodities to ensure equitable prices for farmers. Agricultural leaders began to favor federal marketing controls that did not excessively expand the government's administrative and regulatory powers—an unlikely possibility.

The success of the Farm Bloc showed legislators from the major agricultural states that the farm lobby could help them realize bipartisan policy agendas, and that alliances with farm groups ensured an organized and reliable bloc of votes on election day. As the agricultural economy continued to decline

after 1926, and as farmers began to demand some form of federal relief, congressmen came to rely on agricultural groups
such as the Farm Bureau for information and advice. By 1926
farm-state lawmakers recognized that the question of federal
intervention in the agricultural economy had become a recur-
rent issue, and wisdom mandated working with the farm
lobby rather than working against it. Simply put, the farm
lobby offered solutions while the major political parties and
Presidents Harding, Coolidge, and Hoover considered farm
problems little more than an annoyance. By the early 1930s
farm-state politicians learned that election to Congress demanded the advocacy of a farm program to help their constituents, with advice from the farm lobby. In late 1932 a
reporter called the farm lobby "the most powerful single-
industry lobby in Washington." Agricultural policy had become an important domain of farm organizations as well as
farm implement and other agricultural companies.

Some Midwestern farmers, however, did not believe that
the Farm Bloc or the Farm Bureau met their immediate economic needs, particularly after the stock market crash of 1929.
As agricultural prices plummeted, farm foreclosures rose, and
many banks that had extended credit to farmers failed. Many
Midwestern farmers responded with "direct action" to try to
survive. The most radical members of the Farmers' Union
were prepared to win by force what their desperate appeals for
economic relief had failed to achieve. Milo Reno was their
leader. By February 1932 many members of the Farmers'
Union were demanding a farm "holiday," when farmers
would neither buy nor sell. This withholding action, Reno believed, would quickly close food-processing plants and empty
grocery store shelves. The goal was federal intervention to
guarantee farmers cost-of-production prices plus a profit of
about 5 percent. Once that happened, farmers would return to
their fields.

The Farmers' Holiday Association, organized on May 3, 1932, and essentially the action arm of the Farmers' Union, called for a farm strike. It began in August as farmers dumped milk in ditches, blocked roads, and skirmished with law enforcement officers. But the "farm holiday" failed largely because the movement in general and the strike in particular had been founded on an incredibly unsound economic assumption—that the farm community could maintain an embargo of all markets. Most farmers could not participate for long in such a movement. They had to sell commodities to support their families. Like everyone else, they had bills to pay. A withholding action added more costs to their already troubled operations. The longer they boycotted the markets, the longer they had to feed their livestock; any commodities they withheld from sale would later flood the market and drive prices down.

The "farm holiday" proved once again that American farmers were too independent and their interests and needs too diverse to support a large, united organization indefinitely. They would prove this axiom true again during the administration of Franklin D. Roosevelt and would finally recognize the value of organizing by commodity rather than by vocation or geography. The Farmers' Holiday Association also showed that farmers could not hold together to achieve radical goals by radical means. In the end the Holiday Association could not control enough markets in the Midwest to force major price increases, and the organization held no appeal to farmers in other sections of the nation.

THE MCNARY-HAUGEN PLAN

The post–World War I agricultural recession marked the beginning of a new age in the relationship between farmers and the federal government. Many farmers now sought more than governmental regulation of corporations; they wanted government intervention in the agricultural economy to raise farm prices. By 1924 agricultural leaders, the Farm Bureau, and farmers had reached agreement on a plan to increase prices, restore purchasing power, and improve the standard of living of farm men and women. They called it the McNary-Haugen plan, after Senator Charles McNary of Oregon and Representative Gilbert N. Haugen of Iowa, who introduced the bill in Congress. The McNary-Haugen plan called for the federal government to calculate the amount of certain commodities needed for domestic consumption and to sell the surplus abroad at world prices. As a result, supporters of this plan argued, domestic prices would increase behind the protective tariff to parity levels, providing the purchasing power that farmers had enjoyed from 1909 to 1914. Any losses incurred by the federal government would be covered by an "equalization fee," to cover the difference between the domestic price paid and the world price received when the government sold the surplus. Farmers would benefit to the degree that the domestic price, less the equalization fee, would be higher than the domestic price without dumping the surplus on the world market. Although the McNary-Haugen plan authorized the creation of an agency to buy and sell surplus commodities abroad, it did not authorize the federal government to purchase and store commodities to force a price increase on the world market.

Although Congress first considered the McNary-Haugen plan in 1924, it did not pass the act until 1927 and 1928—but President Calvin Coolidge vetoed it both times. Coolidge did not believe the federal government should intervene in the agricultural economy to influence prices. The McNary-Haugen plan, he contended, would help grain farmers at the expense of dairy farmers who purchased grain for feed, and would encourage grain farmers to increase production and

thereby worsen the surplus problem. Coolidge also believed
the equalization fee was an unconstitutional tax on farmers,
and that the program would create an expensive, "cancerous"
bureaucracy. Instead Coolidge favored cooperative marketing
to improve agricultural prices. Cooperatives, he believed,
could withhold the commodities of their members and sell
them in an orderly fashion that would maintain prices at satisfactory levels. When the Farm Bureau angrily rebuked the
president for vetoing the McNary-Haugen bill, congressmen
took notice of the potential political power of the organization.
The support of agricultural groups suddenly became more
important for congressmen than party solidarity, especially
after the farm lobby made support of the McNary-Haugen
Bill the litmus test for agricultural relief and proved its power
at the polls.

Despite the failure of McNary-Haugen, the debate over the
plan proved to be a turning point in American history because
farmers began the political movement for a federal agricultural program that would resolve price and income problems.
Many leaders and farmers now contended that the federal
government must regulate the agricultural economy beyond
its work through the USDA to make farmers more efficient
and productive.

THE AGRICULTURAL MARKETING ACT

President Herbert Hoover, on the other hand, believed that farmers should also help themselves through voluntary agreements and cooperative action. Rather than use the
power of the federal government to fix prices, Hoover contended that agriculture had become "an extraordinarily highly
competitive industry" where producers outnumbered buyers.
Farmers therefore received "minimum" prices according to
the laws of supply and demand. He also argued that the "log-

ical" solution to surplus production and low prices was for farmers to sell "through more concentrated channels with resources to regulate . . . the supply to demand." Hoover advocated "concentrated control" through centralized commodity associations, which the federal government would help organize and support. To achieve this goal, Hoover asked Congress to pass the Agricultural Marketing Act, which he signed into law on June 15, 1929.

Both Hoover and Congress intended this legislation "to promote the effective merchandising of agricultural commodities in interstate and foreign competition, so that the industry of agriculture will be placed on a basis of economic equality with other industries." Hoover referred to the act as "the most important measure ever passed by Congress in aid of a single industry." Most agricultural leaders, farmers, politicians, and businessmen showed less enthusiasm, but *Wallace's Farmer* spoke for many in declaring that the act was "not the bill farmers wanted, but they are not captious about methods; what they want is results. They want to be assured of an increased share in the national income. If the Hoover plan does this, they will be satisfied, and will gladly give Hoover the credit he would deserve."

The Agricultural Marketing Act authorized the federal government to loan money to agricultural cooperatives from a $500 million revolving fund. The cooperatives would in turn make loans to association members to help them meet expenses while they held their commodities off the market until prices rose, or until they chose to sell their commodities in an "orderly" fashion and thereby avoid swamping the market at harvest times with price-depressing surpluses. The act also created the Federal Farm Board, the first agricultural "action" agency. Hoover believed the "fundamental purpose" of the Farm Board should be to "build up farmer-owned and farmer-controlled institutions for marketing the farmers' crops." As the agricultural economic crisis worsened, however, Hoover's hopes that the Agricultural Marketing Act and the Farm Board would create large national associations of commodity cooperatives vanished.

The Farm Board responded to the continuing crisis by creating stabilization corporations for wheat and cotton to bail out the cooperatives that had purchased too much of these commodities at high prices. These stabilization corporations had the authority to purchase unusually large surpluses of wheat and cotton to keep prices from falling still further. By 1931 the Farm Board, through the stabilization corporations, had spent all its funds to purchase 257 million bushels of wheat and 3.4 million bales of cotton.

The Farm Board did not have the financial resources to ease substantially the agricultural crisis. Its $500 million went to aid cooperatives and increase agricultural prices for targeted commodities, but agricultural prices soon fell below the loan values, and cooperatives failed across the nation. World markets and prices as well as domestic and international business cycles determined the stability of agricultural prices and the prosperity of farmers. Farmers, acting individually or collectively, could not improve their economic situation.

When the Farm Board terminated its operations, wheat and cotton prices fell still further. If nothing else, the failure of the Farm Board and agricultural crop stabilization proved that cooperative marketing would not solve the farm problem. More important, the Farm Board warned, "Prices cannot be kept at a fair level unless production is adjusted to meet market demands." It urged farmers to reduce production, but to no avail.

The Agricultural Marketing Act marked the first attempt by the federal government to develop a comprehensive agricultural policy. But it proved entirely ineffective because a major depression wrecked the national economy just six months after Congress approved the legislation. Between 1929 and 1932 agricultural commodity prices declined from an index of 93 to 58, a 37 percent drop. Gross farm income declined from $13.8 to $6.5 billion, or by 52 percent. Per capita farm income fell from $945 to $304 annually. Rural income averaged only 70 percent of that of manufacturing workers while land values declined by half during those years. Wheat exports decreased from 354 million to 143 million bushels, while cotton exports fell in value from approximately $2.5 billion to $1 billion, and meat exports declined from $246 million to $81 million. Domestic food and fiber consumption also plunged.

In 1931, as cotton farmers produced the second-largest and wheat farmers the third-largest crops in history, prices fell accordingly. Between 1929 and 1932 the average price for wheat fell from $1.03 to 38 cents per bushel; corn dropped from about 80 cents to 32 cents per bushel; cotton declined from nearly 17 cents to 5 cents per pound. Hog prices plummeted from $12.93 to $6.13 per hundredweight. Meanwhile the prices that farmers paid declined more slowly than the prices that they received. Bills and interest payments became more difficult if not impossible, and many men and women lost their farms.

Hoover pleaded with farmers for voluntary reduction of their planted acreage, which he believed would work to increase prices. But in 1932, with cotton prices falling to 5 cents per pound, wheat dropping to less than 20 cents per bushel on some markets, and hogs declining to 3 cents per pound, farmers responded to the price collapse by trying to produce still more. They reasoned that if most farmers did not reduce production, those who did so would be penalized—they would have less product to sell. Consequently farmers did not respond to Hoover's "Grow Less, Get More" campaign. They simply could not control production and prices in the same

way U.S. Steel controlled its market. Farmers were too diverse, and so were their needs, costs, and reliance on domestic
and international markets. Facing bankruptcy and foreclosure, they turned to the federal government in growing numbers. Thus the most important legacy of the Agricultural
Marketing Act was its clear demonstration that the farm problem could not be solved through marketing reform.

By the early 1920s farmers and their agrarian supporters and
lobbying organizations, such as the American Farm Bureau
Federation, had achieved modest government action for the
benefit of agriculture. But government involvement still emphasized regulation to protect farmers from abusive corporations. Farmers favored government regulation of business
because it left them relatively independent and free to compete
fairly and maintain their individualism. Yet in the 1920s many
farmers also sought government support for agricultural cooperatives and price controls through various marketing techniques, which culminated in the federal government's first
attempt to regulate agricultural prices.

Attempting to solve economic difficulties through cooperative action did not work because not all farmers participated.
Farmers had different economic interests that prevented them
from acting together across commodities and regions and even
among themselves as specialized producers. At the same time
the federal government could not coerce farmers to follow the
rules of voluntary production and marketing programs. Cooperatives that served farmers who produced perishable products such as fruits and milk had greater success, because
perishable commodities cannot be held off the market. By
1921 the California Fruit Growers Exchange, for example,
controlled 73 percent of the state's crop. But grain cooperatives
could not control production. Although 511 grain cooperatives

served farmers in the Midwest by 1921, no cooperative could sufficiently control the market to influence prices. By 1924 only 10 percent of the grain farmers marketed their crops through cooperatives.

Although the federal government supported cooperatives after 1920, many agricultural leaders wanted greater federal economic aid to farmers. The U.S. Wheat Growers Association and the Oklahoma Wheat Growers Association, for example, rejected the argument that cooperatives could raise farm prices merely by regulating the flow of agricultural commodities into the marketplace. Both organizations contended that only the federal government could guarantee cost-of-production prices and a "reasonable profit." Yet until agricultural prices collapsed in the early 1930s, farmers failed to organize with enough force to achieve direct federal intervention in the agricultural economy. Instead they skirted the edges of such regulation with the Fordney-McCumber tariff of 1922 and the Hawley-Smoot tariff of 1930, which had no impact on prices of products of which there was an exportable surplus, and by efforts to reduce supplies available for domestic consumption through the McNary-Haugen plan.

Herbert Hoover had hoped that government aid for cooperative marketing would prevent further large-scale federal intervention into the farm economy. He wanted the federal government to function as the coordinator of marketing programs and as a partner with cooperative organizations. But with the onset of the depression in 1929, many farmers sought government regulation and administration of farm programs, and they were prepared to sacrifice freedom of action for profitability. Hoover knew that a regulatory state would require farmers to meet certain reciprocal obligations regarding matters of production control, price supports, and agricultural credit, and he opposed this expansion of state power. Yet his

Agricultural Marketing Act, though a practical failure, marked the beginning of unprecedented government involvement in the agricultural economy.

When Franklin Roosevelt was inaugurated in March 1933, farmers were experiencing the lowest agricultural prices and income since the late nineteenth century. In 1925, when a farmer received $1.50 for a bushel of wheat, he had needed 6,700 bushels to pay off a $10,000 mortgage. In 1933, when the price fell to 30 cents per bushel, he needed more than 33,300 bushels to meet the debt. By Inauguration Day in 1933 farmers had only half the purchasing power they had enjoyed from 1909 to 1914. The Farmers' Holiday movement had lost its energy in the Midwest, where it had emerged with explosive force. Across the nation farmers awaited the actions of a new president. Many of them now looked to the federal government to improve agricultural conditions.

3

The New Deal

ON INAUGURATION DAY, March 4, 1933, the newly elected President Franklin Delano Roosevelt confronted the worst economic depression in American history. Farmers faced the most severe economic situation and lowest agricultural prices since the 1890s. Roosevelt did not believe that Herbert Hoover's policy of providing modest financial support for cooperatives and calling for voluntary production controls would ease the farm crisis. Instead, with typical optimism and measured determination, he promised hope and relief. "This great nation will endure as it has endured, will revive and will prosper. So . . . let me assert my firm belief that the only thing we have to fear is fear itself—nameless, unreasoning, unjustified terror which paralyzes needed efforts to convert retreat into advance." While directing these thoughts to the entire nation, Roosevelt also addressed farm men and women across the country when he spoke of the need for "definite efforts to raise the values of agricultural products."

Farmers hoped for the best and had reason for optimism in the wake of Roosevelt's campaign statements. Roosevelt declared that he had a "very practical and personal interest in the farm problem" and that he was "willing to try things out until we get something that works." He spoke of restoring agricultural purchasing power by increasing farm prices, protecting farm property from foreclosure, and stimulating foreign trade. Farmers not only wanted to hear that message; they believed such actions were essential for their survival.

Overproduction and a shrinking international market had driven down agricultural prices. California continued to symbolize the successful large-scale production of fruit and vegetable crops based on extensive landholdings, cheap irrigation, and migrant labor. Across the Midwest farm men and women watched helplessly as prices fell for corn, hogs, and dairy products, while drought and dust storms inflicted the worst environmental disaster yet recorded in the history of the Great Plains. In the South, sharecropping and the crop lien system combined to impoverish a region where one contemporary observed that farming was "a world in which survival depended on raw courage, a courage born out of desperation and sustained by a lack of alternatives."

THE AGRICULTURAL ADJUSTMENT ADMINISTRATION

Roosevelt moved quickly by calling Congress into special session on March 9. Later known as the "Hundred Days" Congress, it dealt with many economic issues that indicated forethought, understanding, and action as well as poor judgment, inadequate planning, and haste on the part of the Roosevelt administration. By the time Congress adjourned on June 16, 1933, it had passed some of the most unprecedented and long-lasting legislation in American history. For the next three years it continued to do so, especially by legislating farm programs for both immediate relief and long-term recovery. Henry A. Wallace, secretary of agriculture, provided much of the leadership for agricultural reform. Supported by a group of "agricultural fundamentalists," Wallace believed that a strong national economy depended on a prosperous agricultural economy. He contended that a crop-reduction program would end the surplus problem and boost commodity prices, and he proposed a far-reaching program to achieve those goals. On May 12 Congress passed the Agricultural Adjustment Act, which created the Agricultural Adjustment Administration (AAA) as an agency of the U.S. Department of Agriculture (USDA) to administer a program designed to decrease agricultural surpluses on seven commodities—wheat, cotton, corn, rice, tobacco, hogs, and dairy products. The AAA was thus committed to a philosophy of production control. Through it the federal government assumed responsibility for the general welfare of at least a portion of the agricultural community.

The AAA targeted these seven "basic agricultural commodities" for several reasons. First, changes in their prices strongly influenced the prices of other commodities. Second, each of them was running a surplus, and the demand and price for each had fallen substantially. Agricultural experts considered the producers of these export commodities in worse financial condition than farmers who produced other commodities for the domestic market. Third, these commodities required some processing before human consumption. Consequently the production and distribution of their manufactured products could be easily monitored and regulated.

Ultimately the AAA intended the crop-reduction program to increase prices to the parity levels of 1909–1914. It aimed to achieve this parity by balancing production and consumption through a voluntary program that paid farmers to produce less. Funds to support this program and to pay farmers for reducing production would come from taxes on the processors of agricultural commodities, such as textile and flour mills, tobacco companies, and meat processors. The amount that a farmer received to reduce production would be based in part

on the difference between a government-determined price
and the market price—that is, a "fair exchange value minus
the current price."

The AAA adjustment program did not necessarily seek a
return to pre–World War I prices. Rather, agency officials
hoped it would enable farmers who sold the same amount of
the seven basic commodities in 1933 as in 1914 to purchase the
same amount of manufactured goods. Consequently the Roosevelt administration wanted the AAA to return a fair share of
the national income to farmers, who would use that income to
stimulate the economy by purchasing manufactured goods.
The AAA program, then, had two fundamental objectives
based on the law of supply and demand. The first was to increase income toward parity, through "benefit payments" to
farmers for reducing production. The AAA contended that
these benefit payments could be considered "a form of compensation by the rest of society to farmers for their service in
supplying food and raw materials." The second goal was to reduce production to bring these selected commodities in balance with demand and thereby increase prices.

Accomplishing these objectives depended, of course, on the
success of the commodity-reduction programs, the weather,
and the amount of commodities produced by nonparticipating
farmers. Farmers who chose not to sign contracts pledging to
reduce their acreage could plant as many acres or produce as
much wheat, pork, or milk as they chose; but they would be at
the mercy of market forces and prices, and they would not receive marketing or monetary help from the federal government. Participating farmers who exceeded or ignored their
crop allotments would also be disqualified from receiving benefit payments. In essence the federal government forced farmers to participate in the commodity-reduction program,
because without AAA payments they had little hope of en-
during their economic situation until better times returned.

The federal government guaranteed at least modest income for reducing production.

AAA officials believed that income adjustment was the most important aspect of their program. They expected to pay benefits for three years (1933–1935) to producers who signed contracts to restrict production. Participating farmers would receive a "benefit" or "adjustment" payment based on their production during the base period from 1928 to 1932, which the AAA used for calculation. (The tobacco allotment, however, was based on the period from 1919 to 1929, in order to increase the parity price by 17 percent.) This was considerable insurance for farmers because they would receive at least some income for their crops, hogs, and dairy products provided they agreed to reduce production. AAA officials believed the program would give cooperating farmers immediate parity prices for the amount of their commodity consumed in the United States. Eventually, when supply and demand moved into balance, the farmer would receive a parity price for the entire crop, number of hogs, or pounds of milk sold at the marketplace without government subsidy. Thus farmers would benefit from the AAA program in three ways. First, they would receive cash payments from the federal treasury. Second, commodity prices would increase to tariff levels as surpluses declined. Third, the quality of farm life and the standard of living would improve as agricultural prices and income increased.

The work of the AAA is best illustrated by its effect on cotton, wheat, and corn-hog farmers. The AAA launched its cotton reduction program first because one-third of the nation's farmers lived in the South. And there approximately 5 million whites and 3 million African Americans worked as sharecroppers or rented land as tenant farmers. In 1932 cotton prices had fallen to 4.6 cents per pound after the near-record harvest of 13 million bales. With farmers needing approximately 13 cents per pound for parity, they had less than half the purchasing power they had enjoyed from 1909 to 1914. Their income in 1932 had fallen by two-thirds, to $500 million. Yet low prices and large supplies did not prevent cotton farmers from planting even more acreage. In 1933 they seeded 40 million acres, an 11 percent increase over the preceding year. They did so, as one USDA official explained, because "Growers felt driven, despite the disastrously low price of their staple crop, to increase the acreage devoted to it. They had no other cash crops to which they could profitably turn, and necessity to grow something for revenue was compelling."

By the time the AAA became law, half the cotton crop had been planted. Consequently acreage allotments for crop reduction could not be met without plowing up a portion of the newly seeded crop. Nonetheless Agriculture Secretary Wallace moved quickly to implement the program, authorizing the AAA to contract with 1 million farmers to plow under from one-fourth to one-half of their cotton, or more than 10.4 million acres. This action would remove some 3 million bales from the 1933 harvest. Participation ranged from a high of 79 percent of the cotton farmers in Louisiana to a low of 50 percent in North Carolina. Wallace wrote, "To have to destroy a growing crop is a shocking commentary on our civilization. I could tolerate it only as a cleaning up of the wreckage from the old days of unbalanced production." One South Carolinian called the great cotton plow-up the "most gigantic agricultural mass movement ever undertaken."

During the next two crop years the AAA sought to reduce cotton production by 40 percent based on 1928–1932 productivity. For the removal of an approved number of acres, the AAA paid the farmer between $7 and $20 per acre, depending on the productivity of the land. The parity payment depended on the market price of cotton and the average productivity of the acreage harvested during the base period. Sharecroppers and tenant farmers, however, seldom received any portion of the benefit checks; the courts ruled that they were not party to the contracts between landowners and the AAA. The reduction of cotton acreage also meant that fewer sharecroppers and tenant farmers were needed on the land. Indeed, contrary to paragraph 7 of the Agricultural Adjustment Act, planters and other landowners often evicted their tenants and sharecroppers, refusing to allow them to remain in their homes with garden plots that would enable them to meet basic food needs.

By paying farmers to raise less cotton, the AAA also encouraged mechanization, because the landowners often took their checks and bought tractors and other equipment. Thus the AAA began the great enclosure movement in Southern agriculture whereby landowners released their sharecroppers and tenants, combined small farms into large fields, removed houses and fences, and used tractors, cultivators, and mechanical planters to plow, seed, and weed the cotton crop. Then, at harvest time, the landowners hired back many of their old sharecroppers and tenants as day laborers to pick the cotton. When they were not needed, the Federal Emergency Relief Administration offered these workers emergency assistance, essentially providing the "furnish" previously obtained from planters and country merchants.

The AAA cotton-reduction program benefited large-scale landowners and planters, who received guaranteed income for removing their acreage from production. But the program drove thousands of men, women, and children, both black and white, from the land without any provision for their most basic needs. Although the AAA had intended to improve agricultural conditions for cotton farmers, it made life worse for the sharecroppers and tenants who lived in desperation and without hope. By aiding capital-intensive landowners at the expense of sharecroppers and tenants, who comprised about half the agricultural population of the South, the AAA brought radical change to Southern agriculture.

In 1934 the Cotton Section of the AAA realized that landlords were not sharing their acreage reduction money with their tenants. In order to ensure that the farmers who actually raised cotton received the income intended for reducing production, officials in the Cotton Section required landowners in their 1934 and 1935 contracts to distribute acreage-reduction payments equally among their tenants, and to allow tenants who were no longer needed because of the acreage reductions "to continue in the occupancy of their houses on [the] farm, rent free, for the years 1934 and 1935." Although these provisions ensured a semblance of equity and kept displaced tenants and sharecroppers close by for daily wage labor, they had little effect on landowners who ignored the regulation and continued to keep the AAA checks for themselves. Within the AAA a major division developed between those who wished to protect the tenants and sharecroppers and keep them on the land, and those who favored acreage reduction, mechanization, and government support of large-scale, capital-intensive farmers. In 1935, when the AAA's legal section ruled that landowners had to keep their tenants, Secretary Wallace disagreed and fired the "radicals" who supported that action and philosophy in the agency. He thereby assured government support of the planter class.

The Agricultural Adjustment Act provided little aid for sharecroppers and tenant farmers, who were the closest group of farmers this nation has had to a peasant class. They existed in a culture of poverty, but the AAA emphasized economic aid based on commodities rather than on the needs of a certain group as a class. The AAA was not concerned with the survival of poor farmers. Like the USDA in general, the AAA considered them inefficient and incapable of meeting the agricultural needs of the American people.

The more militant sharecroppers believed that the landowners had a "moral obligation" to share their benefit checks. When they continued to refuse, a group of sharecroppers in northeastern Arkansas organized the Southern Tenant Farmers' Union (STFU) in July 1934, hoping to use their strength in numbers to prevent the landowners from evicting tenants as they reduced their cotton acreage. Led by Clay East and H. L. Mitchell, the Southern Tenant Farmers' Union grew to approximately thirty thousand members as it spread into seven states. The landowners responded with mass evictions and continued to use their AAA checks to consolidate or enclose their farms, purchase tractors, and hire released sharecroppers as day laborers. Because the AAA made the landowners the administrators of the program at the county level, the sharecroppers could not receive a fair hearing for their grievances. As a result, the number of sharecroppers and tenant farmers began to decline significantly as the landowners released them. In this sense the AAA accomplished an unintended reform: the restructuring of land use. Certainly the AAA had not intended to alter the relationship between landowners and tenants, nor to help sharecroppers and tenants (dealing with several million landless farmers would have been a bureaucratic nightmare). Consequently the AAA increased human suffering by driving the most desperate and impoverished farm men and women, white and black, from the land.

Income adjustment was also the most important aspect of the AAA's wheat program. Participating farmers would receive a "benefit" or "adjustment" payment of 28 to 30 cents per bushel for a portion of their 1933–1934 crop. This payment would be made on 54 percent of a farmer's average production for the base period 1928–1932. AAA officials considered this percentage the farmer's domestic allotment. For example, if a farmer had planted an average of 100 acres during the base period, with an average yield of 10 bushels per acre, he would receive a minimum of 28 cents per bushel on his domestic allotment of 540 bushels. He could also sell his total crop at the prevailing market rate. Although participation required the farmer to reduce the acreage of his next crop by 15 percent, the AAA wheat program provided insurance that drought-stricken wheat farmers would receive at least some income from their crop.

Many wheat farmers used their benefit checks to meet essential needs and pay bills, bank loans, and taxes, and thereby improve their credit rating. Farm families considered this money a windfall, and farm women played a major role in determining how it was spent. But the benefit payments could not meet all the basic financial needs of a farm family because a large part of the money was needed to purchase seed wheat and pay planting expenses, such as the cost of gasoline for tractors and feed for horses. Even so, wheat farmers welcomed the AAA benefit payments.

Despite this enhanced income, the AAA wheat program made only a slight reduction in planted acreage. Wheat farmers often attempted to rent as much land as possible in order to plant more wheat and make up for their losses to drought and the adjustment program. Meanwhile they received AAA payments for reducing acreage on their own lands. More effective in reducing output was the drought. It contributed to a rise in wheat prices from a low of 47 cents per bushel in 1931 to 88 cents per bushel in 1934 on the Kansas City market, earning Kansas farmers an estimated $275.4 million. AAA benefit payments raised that income by another third, or $98.6 million.

In August 1933 the AAA also confronted the problem of low hog prices through a purchase-and-slaughter program designed to remove the price-depressing surplus from the market. By so doing the AAA earned the criticism of consumers who rightfully charged that people were starving while the federal government wasted food in order to prop up farm income. Agriculture Secretary Wallace said the federal government would solve this "paradox of want in the midst of plenty" by purchasing "from those who had too much, in order to give to those who had too little." Many citizens nonetheless attacked the federal government for this policy, even if the pork was used for food relief. Wallace insisted that "no one would go hungry or ragged because of any of our adjustment programs." The hog purchase program was a lightning rod for supporters and critics of the AAA. The farmers, however, cared little about those who argued against the program. They wanted government checks, and they believed the primary job of the federal government was to stabilize the hog market. After that it could use surplus pork for food relief.

The AAA "pig-buying program" removed more than 6 million hogs from farms and markets. Many of these hogs were used for fertilizer and lard, but the government purchased an additional 2 million head for distribution through food relief programs. Soon the income of hog producers increased 10 percent. In the autumn of 1933 the AAA expanded its purchase program by offering contracts to farmers who pledged to reduce their corn acreage by 20 to 30 percent and their hog production by 25 percent in return for government benefit payments. Organizational difficulties at the county level prevented more than a fourth of corn farmers from participating, but approximately 70 percent of the hog producers signed contracts to reduce production.

The hog program encouraged cattlemen to call upon President Roosevelt to use his "extraordinary powers" to include them in the AAA program and purchase 2 million head "at a price commensurate with debts" for slaughter and distribution as canned beef through the Red Cross. The American National Livestock Association also urged "prompt action by the government" and asked it to purchase 75 million cattle to support prices and remove surpluses under the guise of food relief. Dairy farmers too joined the cause, asking the federal government to purchase "low-producing dairy cows" for food relief purposes. In November 1933 the Federal Emergency Relief Corporation, which coordinated the relief activities of the AAA and the Federal Emergency Relief Administration, responded by agreeing to purchase 15 million pounds of beef per month for relief. In May 1934 this program expanded with the creation of the Drought Relief Service, which continued the cattle purchase program on the Great Plains. For farmers, the tradeoff was that the federal government required participating livestock raisers to sign production-control contracts. Although the cattle purchase program was not part of the AAA, it had the same goals—provide income and remove surplus product.

In the autumn of 1933 the AAA began mailing several hundred thousand checks to farmers who had agreed to reduce production of the targeted seven commodities. These funds, for both land reduction and price supports, were the first substantial income many farmers had received in two years. The federal government now had a new relationship with farmers; the AAA had put the government in the business of production control. Most important, the AAA committed the government to the principle of guaranteeing parity prices for farmers. Congress had approved the Agricultural Adjustment Act on the premise that farmers needed the federal government to help them deal with other economic groups as an equal, rather than from their previous position of disadvantage or weakness. For many farmers, participation in the AAA program of production controls and price supports meant the difference between having an income or going on relief.

Although the federal government imposed the AAA program on the farmers of key commodities, the organization of the agency indicates the participatory regulation that characterized many New Deal programs. The AAA's wheat-reduction program offers a good example of the decentralized, locally controlled organizational structure that made participating farmers part of the regulatory process. The success of the voluntary wheat-reduction program depended on participating farmers not only reducing their planted acreage but also refraining from increasing production on unrestricted acres with heavy applications of fertilizer. To guarantee compliance the AAA required "certificates of performance" from the county committees, certifying that each wheat farmer had reduced his acreage as required. To aid the committee the AAA's state wheat agent appointed "farm allotment supervisors" to visit the participating farmers and inspect their fields. In principle the Wheat Section appointed these inspectors from a list of names submitted by each county production-control association. In practice the county association chose its inspectors, who were then approved by the Wheat Section. Thus there was considerable local control and administration of the program. The supervisors visited each contracted farmer and measured his seeded acres to ensure that over-planting had not occurred, either accidentally or intentionally.

The AAA also considered the county extension agents its "shock troops" for organizing and administering the program at the local level. The agents made direct contacts with farmers for the AAA, and they provided leadership for organizing county production-control associations. The county agent worked with representatives of agricultural organizations and county governing officials to appoint a temporary committee (usually the leading wheat growers) to urge local wheat farmers to meet and organize a production-control association and participate in the AAA program. The elected directors of this association handled applications, allotments, contracts, payments, and compliance, and reported to the Wheat Section of the AAA. The officers of the production-control association usually had been active in agricultural organizations, farm cooperatives, and community activities.

Similarly the AAA permitted the dairy industry to develop plans that regulated the marketing agreements between dairy associations and cooperatives and distributors, subject to agency approval. As farmers overwhelmingly and voluntarily signed up for production-control programs, they became part of the local program administration and fostered a more democratic bureaucracy.

THE SUPREME COURT AND THE AGRICULTURAL ADJUSTMENT ACT

Opponents of the AAA cared little for the program's monetary boost to farmers and the agricultural economy. During 1935 they increasingly challenged the constitutionality of the Agricultural Adjustment Act, particularly the tax on processors. Ultimately the attack by conservatives on the agency proved successful. On January 6, 1936, the U.S. Supreme Court declared the AAA unconstitutional on the grounds that Congress had no authority to regulate agricultural production by levying a processing tax to pay for the program. The Court contended that the processing tax was not a real tax but rather an agricultural production-control device that was voluntary in name only. In the Court's 6 to 3 decision, Justice Owen Roberts, writing for the majority, held that the benefit payments to farmers were intended to "coerce" them to accept regulation of the agricultural economy by the federal government. The Court did not rule specifically that federal regulation of the agricultural economy was unconstitutional, only that Congress could not do so under the taxing power granted by the Constitution. Put differently, the Court affirmed that the federal government could use tax funds to aid the nation's general welfare, but it did not consider crop benefit payments to farmers in that category.

The Roosevelt administration moved quickly in response to the Supreme Court's decision, because many farmers had come to depend on their allotment checks for daily living expenses and to pay bills, and because 1936 was a presidential election year. The administration worked rapidly to achieve congressional approval of the Soil Conservation and Domestic Allotment Act, which became law on February 29, 1936. Although policymakers still emphasized the increase of farm income, this new legislation authorized the AAA to pay farmers for planting soil-conserving, rather than soil-depleting, crops. Of course the soil-depleting crops were those the USDA considered in surplus. If, for example, farmers could plant alfalfa where cotton or wheat had previously grown, the federal government would pay them to do so from the general revenue fund, not by assessing a special tax.

More important, the new legislation shifted the policy goal from parity prices to parity income by reestablishing "the [1909–1914] ratio between the purchasing power of the net income per person on farms and that of the income per person not on farms." This shift in the basis for payments proved more equitable. It enabled small-scale farmers to share in the distribution of funds, because they could now receive income for practicing soil-conservation techniques on any part of their crop and pasture lands, in contrast to the reduction of crop acreage alone. This policy contrasted sharply with the first AAA which primarily aided the large-scale farmers, who received most of the allotment money because they owned the most acres to remove from production. Thus federal payments to farmers continued, and in November farmers cast a strong

majority vote for Roosevelt. Al Smith, the defeated Democratic presidential nominee in 1928, said they did so because
nobody wanted to shoot Santa Claus.

In 1938 Congress institutionalized this policy by passing a
new Agricultural Adjustment Act that continued to emphasize production control through acreage allotments and payments for specified conservation practices. The act used the
term *parity* for the first time in legislation. It also provided
price-supporting loans through the Commodity Credit Corporation. And it authorized the secretary of agriculture to establish marketing quotas if he believed the production of
certain crops would cause price-depressing surpluses. In that
event he could, upon approval of two-thirds of the farmers
who participated in the specific crop program, limit the sales
of that crop on the domestic market in order to help maintain
an acceptable price. Secretary Wallace believed the AAA of
1938 would create an "ever normal granary," that is, ensure
stable supplies and prices from year to year, during good times
and bad. The act also introduced crop insurance for wheat
farmers, which soon expanded to provide protection for farmers who raised other crops. Perhaps more important, the AAA
of 1938 made the agricultural allotment and payment programs permanent. They no longer depended on special annual
appropriations but rather became part of the normal pro-
grammatic budgeting process of the USDA.

In retrospect the AAA programs gave landowning farmers
much-needed financial support. At the same time the USDA
recognized that too many farmers (including tenants and
sharecroppers) remained on the land for all of them to prosper.
The agency was committed to encouraging small-scale farmers to leave agriculture. The benefit payments that landowners shared with their tenants—if they shared them at
all—were too small to improve the tenants' standard of living
or to keep many of them on the land.

Problems of drought and economic depression could not be solved quickly. No one had ever grappled with the difficulty of providing monetary aid to farmers in return for withholding production. Even so, when the aid to farmers is considered along with other support programs such as the Federal Emergency Relief Administration, the Works Progress Administration, and the Farm Security Administration, the AAA helped many farmers endure drought and economic hard times until the rains returned and World War II increased both demand and prices. In this context the AAA proved to be one of the most important and popular agencies in the lives of farmers during the 1930s. It also marked the beginning of the federal government's active role in regulating the agricultural economy. Certainly the AAA laid the foundation for an agricultural policy that affected nearly every farmer until the late twentieth century. Whether or not they approved of government intervention in agriculture, farmers came to depend on AAA-inspired policy that built on the income-generating, allotment, and marketing methods introduced during the 1930s. They would be wedded to that policy for the remainder of the century.

THE COMMODITY CREDIT CORPORATION

While the AAA was attempting to reduce production, the Commodity Credit Corporation (CCC), created by executive order of the president in October 1933, helped end the "furnishing" system in the South. The CCC provided price-supporting loans for cotton and wheat, and later for other commodities, at 60 to 70 percent of the parity price in order to keep those crops off the market and thereby help stabilize if not increase prices. For example, the CCC loaned money at the rate of 10 cents per pound for cotton and stored the farmer's crop at 4 percent interest. During the course of the year, if cotton prices rose above the loan rate, the farmer could sell his crop, pay his loan, and pocket the profit. If the price of cotton fell below the loan rate, the farmer forfeited his crop to the CCC and his debt was forgiven.

CCC loans were called "nonrecourse" loans because the agency could not take action against farmers who forfeited their crop, and farmers had no recourse other than to permit the CCC to take their crop if the market price fell below the loan level. Essentially the CCC established a guaranteed price floor which protected farmers from losses greater than their loan indebtedness. No farmer could easily walk away from a federal loan that had no serious ramifications for forfeiture. But farmers who participated in the CCC program had to sign production-control agreements through the AAA to reduce their planted acreage the next year. In 1933 the CCC loaned $160 million on 4.3 million bales of cotton. CCC loans soon became the principal means of supporting farm prices, and the program greatly expanded after World War II.

THE DUST BOWL

In 1931 drought struck the southern Great Plains with unprecedented severity. By spring 1935 the soil was billowing into great clouds called "black blizzards" as the wind eroded fields where wheat, grain sorghum, and grass had once grown in abundance. Drought, dust, and depression became triple plagues for Dust Bowl farmers. As their crops withered under the sun and the wind blew away their topsoil, their income plummeted. Many moved away, but most farmers looked to the federal government for the aid necessary to keep them on the land.

Although the Agricultural Adjustment Act provided the drought-stricken farmers of the southern Great Plains with the most important monetary aid, the federal government for the first time also engaged in planning for agricultural conservation in the Great Plains. In March 1933 the Forest Service began working on a plan to plant trees in shelterbelts to slow the wind on the Great Plains. Although the focus of the project changed several times, by 1942 the Forest Service had planted more than eighteen thousand miles of shelterbelts to help check wind erosion and protect farmsteads. In this work the federal government made agreements with farmers for the use of their lands for tree planting. The Forest Service not only paid farmers a rental fee for the land planted in trees but also paid them to cultivate the plantings. For many farmers these federal payments were welcome income during hard times.

The most optimistic attempt to control the environment of the Great Plains, however, involved the land-use program of the Resettlement and Farm Security administrations. Along with the Soil Conservation Service, these agencies contended that if severely eroded lands could be removed from cultivation and restored to grass, and the blowing rangelands reseeded, the soil could be stabilized, the dust storms ended, and the land returned to a grazing economy under federal control. Accordingly, in 1935 the Resettlement Administration began a land-purchase program to acquire the most severely wind-eroded lands of the Great Plains in order to restore them with grass and the best soil-conservation techniques. The Resettlement Administration and the Farm Security Administration, which assumed this responsibility in 1937, identified severe wind erosion or "problem" areas on the plains and offered to purchase those lands for purposes of restoration. By the time the Soil Conservation Service took over this work in 1938, the land-purchase program had become an unprecedented experiment in state-sponsored environmental and social planning. Since 1960 many of these land utilization projects have been designated national grasslands. Although farmers were not required to sell their lands in project areas, the land-purchase program illustrates another way in which the federal government assumed a regulatory role in American agriculture.

In 1935 the government also created the Soil Conservation Service (SCS) in the Department of Agriculture to help farmers conserve their land. The SCS provided experts and funds to support the application of various wind and water anti-erosion techniques, such as the building of terraces, emergency plowing for erosion control, and the seeding of grass on submarginal lands. The SCS did not believe it had the constitutional authority to require land-use regulations, but the agency asked states to impose those controls. Accordingly the SCS in 1936 drafted a model law for the states, which authorized the creation of soil-conservation districts by local petition and referendum. After districts organized under the guidance of a state soil-conservation committee, and signed a cooperative agreement with the USDA, district supervisors worked on various conservation programs, extended federal financial aid to farmers, signed contracts for specific practices, bought lands for retirement, and formulated land-use ordinances subject to farmer approval.

The Resettlement and Farm Security Administrations

In April 1935 President Roosevelt established the Resettlement Administration (RA) by executive order to assume the rural rehabilitation programs of the Federal Emergency Relief Administration and to help the most destitute farmers, whom one contemporary called the "dispossessed and disinherited." The RA worked to purchase submarginal land and return it to federal domain for the purposes of soil conservation. The agency also tried to rehabilitate farm families by resettling them on better lands, often in newly built homes in model cooperative communities. Although the RA intended to purchase marginal lands and resettle poor farmers on more suitable acreage in other locations, it did not have sufficient funding to develop this aspect of the program beyond a few experimental attempts. In the South, landlords believed that the Resettlement Administration would deplete the labor supply by giving tenants and sharecroppers the opportunity to become landowning farmers, independent of the planters. Even so, by 1936 the RA had aided more than half a million poor farm families by providing money for groceries as well as resettling some on new lands.

In 1937 Congress created the Bankhead-Jones Farm Tenant Act, which authorized the Farm Security Administration. The FSA was designed to reorganize New Deal agricultural programs, including those of the Resettlement Administration. It attempted to reduce farm tenancy and sharecropping by strengthening the financial viability of farm families through "rehabilitation" loans. These loans went to those farmers who could not qualify for credit at traditional lending institutions such as banks and insurance or mortgage companies, but who, the FSA judged, could succeed with credit and supervision. Only those farmers who had exhausted all other forms of credit were eligible to apply for rehabilitation loans. They allowed farmers to buy necessities, such as food, clothing, feed, seed, and fertilizer, in the expectation of making them self-sufficient. Before making the loan, however, the FSA designed a farm management program. It budgeted the farmer's expenses so that he knew how much to spend and still meet his loan and mortgage obligations. Rehabilitation loans were granted to farmers whose operations promised to be self-sustaining, given adequate access to equipment, seed, and livestock. Large-scale landowners in the South particularly resented the FSA because the agency threatened to upset traditional landlord-tenant relations, especially the reliance of tenants and sharecroppers on landowners for credit. Until the

creation of the FSA, the federal government had not become
so involved with individual farm families in planning their
daily lives.

The federal government also provided emergency farm
mortgage assistance with Title II of the Agricultural Adjustment Act. It enabled farmers to avoid foreclosure by providing
liberal funding for the refinancing of loans. The government
also became the chief financing agent for farmers and their cooperatives through the Farm Credit Administration (FCA),
created in 1933 by executive order. Congress supported this
move to consolidate federal agricultural credit activities by
passing the Farm Credit Act, which reorganized federal credit
agencies under the FCA. The FCA purchased farm mortgages from banks and other lenders at discount rates, then re-
financed the mortgages at lower interest rates over a longer
period of time. The FCA also authorized farmer-owned Production Credit Associations to make short- and intermediate-
term loans to enable farmers to purchase livestock,
implements, and supplies. In 1940 FCA loans averaged $1,500.
In addition, Farm Credit Banks supported the marketing,
supply, and service operations of agricultural cooperatives.
The FCA also provided funds to the Federal Land Banks to
enable them to lower interest rates and defer the collection of
principal payments and foreclosures. By the end of 1933 the
FCA had loaned $100 million to help farmers refinance their
mortgages. Without government aid, most of these mortgages
would have been foreclosed. By 1937 the FCA held 40 percent
of all farm mortgages. This agency and Commodity Credit
Corporation became the primary lenders for farmers. In addition to financial aid, the FCA provided low-interest loans to
farmers for crop production, harvesting, and the purchase of
livestock feed, and became the most important agency on
which farmers depended for their credit needs.

THE RURAL ELECTRIFICATION ADMINISTRATION

No federal program changed farm life more fundamentally and positively than the Rural Electrification Administration (REA). Although Congress established the Tennessee Valley Authority in 1933 to provide electric power across a portion of the South, the REA, created by executive order on May 11, 1935, made possible electric service in rural areas across the nation. In 1930 only about 10 percent of the nation's farm homes enjoyed electric service from a central station. The private utility companies had refused to provide service to farms because the revenues did not justify the cost. In order to get electricity to farms, the REA loaned money to rural cooperatives to finance the stringing of power lines, the wiring of homes, and the generating of electricity.

Farmers who organized these electric cooperatives then presented a plan for establishing service, including "area coverage." This ensured that all farms in an area would have access to electric service, with costs equalized over areas that often had low population density. By late 1936 the rural demand for cheap power had translated into nearly 100 co-ops in 26 states that had REA loan contracts. Congress converted the REA from an emergency to a permanent agency and guaranteed funding of $420 million over the next decade. By the late 1930s REA lines had become a common feature across the landscape, and more than 350 REA projects in 45 states provided electric service to almost 1.5 million farms. By the time it was transferred to the jurisdiction of the USDA in 1939 to improve administration, the REA was one of the most successful New Deal agencies. Electricity furnished through the REA brought farm families indoor plumbing, hot water heaters, electric irons and stoves, sewing machines, vacuum cleaners, and refrigerators as well as electric-powered cream separators, feed grinders, heaters, hay elevators, and pumps for water and milk.

THE FARM LOBBY

By the mid-1930s a powerful farm coalition had developed among Southern and Midwestern congressmen. At the same time special commodity groups, such as those representing wheat and corn growers and dairy farmers, had also organized, enabling farmers to wield considerable political power from county government to the offices of the U.S. Department of Agriculture and the halls of Congress. These commodity and sectional interests intended to use their political base to guarantee continued government payments for crop reduction, acreage allotment, and price supports for the most capital-intensive, prosperous, and influential farmers. They did not represent small-scale, lower-class, and marginal agriculturists.

The farm organizations transcended political parties. The American Farm Bureau Federation had no plan to deal with the collapse of the agricultural economy, but it supported the Roosevelt administration's program to control production and increase commodity prices and farm income through the AAA. The Farm Bureau also used its close working relationship with county agents and state extension systems, which it dominated, to help the AAA administer its programs. Its support of the AAA projected power and unity across regions, particularly the Midwest and South. The Farm Bureau also supported the Soil Conservation Service and the Agricultural Adjustment Act of 1938, and claimed to be the "voice of agriculture," though it spoke only for larger-scale commercial producers. It opposed the unionization of labor as well as the Farm Security Administration because the FSA operated independently of the extension service and catered to small-scale, marginal farmers.

In contrast, the leadership of the Farmers' Union at first opposed the AAA, arguing that the agency's programs did not provide sufficient relief. The FU continued to advocate its own cost-of-production-plus-a-profit plan. Some members of the organization, however, supported the AAA because it offered at least some immediate economic relief. In 1937, after several years of infighting and the deaths of its president, John Simpson, and Milo Reno, leader of the Farmers' Holiday Association, which served as the political action arm of the Farmers' Union, the organization cast its support for the AAA.

During the depression decade the Grange supported the AAA crop-reduction program and the consolidation of federal agricultural lending agencies under the Farm Credit Administration. In general, Grange members contended that agricultural problems stemmed from underconsumption rather than overproduction, and they preferred better marketing to crop-reduction programs as a way of improving the farm economy.

No matter which party held the presidency or provided the majority in Congress, the conditions that had made these farm organizations necessary persisted. The members and leadership continued to press their cause for economic relief. In 1937, for example, Agriculture Secretary Wallace told the House Agriculture Committee: "In my observation the farm group has reached the conclusion that as a group it will not abandon the concept of parity price and parity income, no matter what the present situation may be. They will continue to fight for it." Politicians also supported aid to agriculture because the farm vote remained important; representative apportionment had not yet shifted political power to urban areas. Senator Richard B. Russell of Georgia exemplified this reality when he told voters during the 1936 primary election, "The farmers are awake to the fact that my opponent is promising them nothing except to cut off their checks, while I stand for larger benefit checks." Pressure from farmers mandated political support for federal intervention in the agricultural economy.

The farm organizations that lobbied Congress for their constituents kept their members informed about the positions of their elected officials and provided information to politicians about farmers' wants and expectations. The farm organizations shaped, if not determined, the choices and responses of their constituents, and they played an instrumental role in crafting agricultural policy. As a consequence, during the 1930s Republican politicians could not offer a viable alternative to New Deal agricultural programming; they could challenge Democrats only by offering more. In 1938, for example, Republican political contenders pledged to maintain payments but ease crop allotment regulations.

Specialists in the various agencies of the USDA worked with agricultural organizations to develop farm policy. Although the Grange and the Farmers' Union did not support the Farm Bureau on all issues, all joined to demand parity prices and income, concepts that now drove the formulation of agricultural policy—though the best means for achieving these ends remained in dispute. The USDA, through the secretary of agriculture, consistently sought the advice of major farm leaders and their organizations before submitting legislation to Congress. At the same time the farm lobby enjoyed nearly unrestricted access to Congress.

County agents, extension services, and land-grant colleges that supported commercial farmers also spoke with a powerful collective voice when Congress appropriated funds for farm programs. Democratic and Republican politicians knew that termination of the New Deal support programs would cause economic havoc for farm families—with resulting political disaster for themselves and their party. Farmers might depend on the federal government, but through their organizations they controlled much of that dependence and the rewards that came from it.

New Deal agricultural policy thus showed mixed results. New Dealers achieved important economic success by providing direct monetary support to improve farm income through various production, credit, and loan programs. By providing a minimum income to participating farmers, these programs served as the equivalent of minimum-wage legislation. Prices for corn, wheat, and cotton averaged between 50 and 60 percent of parity during the 1930s, but prices increased after the stock market crash of 1929. CCC loans kept supplies off the market and generated farm income for farmers who produced staple crops. Government subsidies also provided a measure of stability on the farm during economic hard times. Even so, high production kept prices from rising anywhere near the parity level, and the AAA and CCC programs encouraged farmers to produce crops that were already in surplus, because they were assured a guaranteed income with no risk for participation. Moreover, New Deal agricultural policy could not prevent production and operating costs from increasing, so the many farm programs could not by themselves make farming profitable. Gross, net, and individual average farm income remained flat between 1930 and 1940, moving from $11.2 to $11.3 billion for gross income; $4.2 to $4.4 billion for net income; and $651 to $706 for average individual net farm income. The parity price index averaged only 81 compared with 83 in 1930.

By World War II many farmers had come to depend on the federal government for acreage-reduction payments as well as low-interest credit, price supports, conservation aid, and rural electrification. Put differently, by 1941 more than a third of gross farm income came from payments for participation in federal programs. Although most farmers disliked production controls, they agreed to them as an emergency measure because they needed the money. Federal funds were the great incentive for participating in the crop-reduction program. Even so, by 1939 farm prices reached only 77 percent of parity, and per capita farm income averaged only 37.5 percent of nonfarm per capita income. Not all commodities were covered by price-support and acreage-reduction programs, and large-scale farmers benefited more than small-scale agriculturists. Surpluses existed for most crops, and overproduction continued to keep prices low despite government programs to reduce production and remove commodities from the market.

Despite the New Deal's experimentation with a host of programs, Secretary Wallace's critics complained in general about the USDA's "policy of scarcity" and the moral wrong of destroying crops, reducing production, and killing livestock in order to aid one group in American society. No one had a solution for the farm problem. Certainly New Deal farm programs failed to reduce production in a controlled manner similar to manufacturing and industrial practices. Millions of farmers had too many diverse interests and needs. Moreover, between 1930 and 1940 the population increased 7 percent but agricultural production rose 12 percent. Nor did New Deal farm policy retire land or reduce production enough to compensate for new developments in science and technology that increased efficiency and production.

Still, the Roosevelt administration confronted the major problem of alleviating human suffering, much of which occurred on farms across the nation. The federal government, primarily through the USDA, acted with both speed and carelessness. It met with both success and failure, the latter caused by contradictory and inequitable programs as well as insufficient funding. The AAA, for example, favored the removal of tenants, sharecroppers, and other inefficient, small-scale farmers from the land. At the same time the Resettlement Administration and the Farm Security Administration provided loans to tenant and other small-scale farmers to help them improve their productivity and *remain* on the land. Landowners with at least some capital benefited from New Deal agricultural programs while sharecroppers and tenant farmers faced exclusion. The farm problem was indeed complex, and the federal government necessarily had to experiment because it had never before attempted to regulate or order the agricultural economy. Most New Deal farm programs achieved a measure of success and improved the lives of farm men, women, and children. Given the circumstances, the federal government achieved about as much as anyone might reasonably have expected in controlling production and increasing farm prices. By World War II the federal government had initiated the primary programs it would use to aid farmers and solve the "farm problem" over the next sixty years.

While the farm population remained stable during the 1930s, its percentage of the total population fell from approximately 25 percent in 1930 to 23 percent in 1940. The number of farms also declined, from 6.2 million to 6.1 million, while the average size increased from 157 to 175 acres. These changes, with the exception of the relative stability of the farm population, marked important trends in American agriculture for the remainder of the century.

Although many farmers had been skeptical about federal intervention in the agricultural economy before the Great Depression, most now considered it an entitlement. The government itself now viewed control of the agricultural economy as a matter of necessity and obligation. It provided more direct economic assistance to farmers than to any other economic or business group. To receive this aid, farmers had to submit to a myriad of government regulations that most agriculturists would once have considered intolerable. By accepting that aid and the ordering of the agricultural economy as both a necessity and a right, farmers lost more freedom and independence, and relied on the federal government more than ever before. The government was now an activist agent in the farm economy. It would maintain its regulatory role until the end of the twentieth century.

4

Prosperity and Decline

FARM MEN AND WOMEN continued to battle low prices and surplus production in the presidential election year of 1940. Although Franklin Roosevelt's New Deal agricultural program had helped many farmers remain on the land, had inaugurated a major soil-conservation program, and had brought electricity to rural families through the Tennessee Valley Authority and the Rural Electrification Administration, low prices and surplus production remained major problems that prevented most farm families from earning a standard of living comparable to city dwellers. Compared to the index period from 1910 to 1914, the ratio of prices received to prices paid averaged only 81, still considerably less than the 1929 ratio of 93. In other words, farmers paid considerably more for everything compared to the prices they received for their commodities. Moreover the farm population had increased from 30.5 million in 1930 to 32.1 million by 1935, as many men and women returned to their family homes when they lost their jobs in the cities as the economy collapsed.

During the 1930s the U.S. Department of Agriculture (USDA), the extension service, and land-grant colleges worked to aid successful farmers who influenced Congress through the major agricultural organizations. These farmers had the capital, land, and technology to make the best use of government aid to survive hard times and eventually prosper. Sharecroppers, tenants, and low-income farmers were essentially ignored by these institutions and organizations because many agricultural officials and leaders considered them too poor, inefficient, and small-scale to improve their farming operations, even with federal support. Within the USDA, the Bureau of Agricultural Economics continued to believe that too many farm men and women remained on the land and contributed to overproduction and low prices. Sharecroppers and tenants seldom voted in the South because of racial and poll tax restrictions, so politicians gave them little attention. The expected return of many young men and women to Southern farms after World War II threatened to make a bad situation worse. Meanwhile, agricultural surpluses of staple commodities remained high because New Deal programs encouraged farmers to produce and sell to the federal government through the Agricultural Adjustment Administration and Commodity Credit Corporation programs. Federal officials were still seeking answers to these problems of the farm economy when the Japanese attacked Pearl Harbor on December 7, 1941.

America's entry into World War II quickly solved the agricultural problems of low prices, overproduction, and excessive farm population. Many men and women left the farms for the military or employment in war-related industries in the cities. Agricultural surpluses soon disappeared as food needs increased for the military and for urban workers. Farm prices rose accordingly. Farmers are historically among the first to profit from war, because it immediately increases the demands of governments for food and fiber. After Congress declared war on Japan, the USDA urged farmers to produce more food products. Farmers had no objections to increasing production, but they wanted the federal government to guarantee parity prices for their efforts. They did not want the government to set minimum prices, which might become maximum prices, as they had for wheat and cotton during World War I. At the same time urban workers feared rapid and exorbitant increases in food costs, and many demanded price controls. Edward O'Neal, president of the American Farm Bureau Federation, told Congress that farmers needed commodity prices not less than 110 percent of parity to compensate for price fluctuations during the year and to ensure an average of 100 percent parity prices. O'Neal argued that consumers had become so used to "buying food at starvation prices that they had forgotten what constitutes fair prices." Farmers believed that city dwellers, particularly workers, who received high wartime wages were the real cause of the inflationary spiral and sought to keep them from earning an adequate income. The time had come for the federal government to correct that inequity.

Congress responded to this demand in January 1942 with the Emergency Price Control Act. It prohibited farm prices from falling below 110 percent of parity. One critic charged that Congress had surrendered to "one of the most greedy and overbearing of all pressure groups—the farm bloc." Another charged that government economic relief for farmers had "degenerated into a grand and glorious racket." Many city dwellers believed that congressional leaders from the agricultural states had exploited "the national emergency to grab everything possible for agriculture while the getting is good." Farm-state leaders responded that their constituents simply wanted a "fair deal."

While consumers complained that the federal government had given favored treatment to agriculture, farmers worried that Congress would impose a ceiling on agricultural prices and a floor under the prices of nonfarm goods and wages. They also feared that high farm prices would collapse into recession once the war ended, similar to the years following

World War I. These fears proved to be warranted when President Roosevelt, in September 1942, asked Congress to control rapidly escalating farm prices. Roosevelt believed some way could be found to place a reasonable ceiling or maximum on farm products which would "enable us also to guarantee to the farmer that he would receive a fair minimum price for his products for one year, or even two years—or whatever period is necessary after the end of the war."

As a result, Congress, with the support of the Farm Bureau, the Grange, and the National Council of Farmer Cooperatives, worked to ease farmers' fears of a postwar recession by amending the Emergency Price Control Act. In October 1942 it set a ceiling on agricultural prices at 100 percent of parity or the highest prices received for commodities between January 1 and September 15, 1942, whichever was higher. Most agricultural prices were increasing rapidly or already exceeded parity, so farmers did not complain. More important, the amendment, introduced by Alabama congressman Henry B. Steagall, guaranteed cotton, corn, wheat, rice, and tobacco farmers price supports at 90 percent of parity for two years after the war ended, through the Commodity Credit Corporation. Farmers participating in the CCC program would still be required to observe acreage and marketing quotas and regulations. The Steagall amendment thus protected farmers against a collapse of farm prices after the war, but it established the principle of high, guaranteed price supports for farmers, which in turn made farmers increasingly reliant on the federal government.

High, guaranteed prices gave many farmers, reared in the agricultural depression of the 1920s and 1930s, the first prosperity they had ever known. In 1942 farm prices averaged 105 percent of parity and reached 113 percent in 1946. Between 1940 and 1945 net cash income for farmers increased from $4.4 billion to $12.3 billion. Average per capita farm net income increased from $706 to $2,063. Although farm income still averaged only 57 percent of the income of everyone else, the war years for most farmers were a time of "milk and honey." Many farmers used their increased earnings to buy more land and equipment, pay debts, and save. Some farmers became financially secure, and more than thirty years later many observers attributed their wealth to the war and the high prices they received then and after, all guaranteed by the federal government. Thereafter farmers would favor maximum production and parity prices as a matter of equity.

During World War II, farmers, particularly the large-scale operators called "growers" in the West, also looked to the federal government to help solve their labor problems. As the military and war industries lured workers from the fields, the farm labor shortage became severe, especially for fruit and vegetable production. At the same time these farmers were attempting to expand production to meet wartime needs and capitalize on high prices. With fewer tractors, plows, and cultivators available (in October 1942 the War Production Board restricted the production of farm machinery to divert steel for military purposes), more growers needed hand labor.

In 1942 the California Citrus Growers Association estimated that half its crop would rot because too few workers were available to pick. The various farm organizations now demanded government help. Congress responded by providing draft deferments for farmers and farm workers who were "necessary to and regularly engaged in an agricultural occupation." Southerners made certain that Congress considered tobacco an "essential crop," thereby exempting tobacco farmers from the draft. Large-scale growers in California also sought to import Mexican farm workers, whom they called "guest workers." By June 1942 the farm labor shortage had become so serious that California's Governor Culbert Olson told Secretary of Agriculture Claude R. Wickard, Secretary of Labor

Francis Perkins, and Secretary of State Cordell Hull that "Without substantial numbers of Mexicans the situation is certain to be disastrous to the entire Victory program." Representatives of the State Department and Mexico then began negotiating an agreement to import Mexican workers, called *braceros,* which became effective in August.

The *bracero* program allowed the importation of Mexican workers for five years. The federal government, under the auspices of the USDA and the U.S. Employment Service, exempted these workers from military service and guaranteed transportation, living expenses, and repatriation. The *braceros* could not be used to replace American workers or to lower wages. The Farm Security Administration (FSA) would negotiate contracts between individual *braceros* and their employers, essentially making the federal government an employer and overseerer of the modern version of the seventeenth-century practice of indentured servitude. L. G. Williams, who supervised the *bracero* program for the Department of Labor, called it "legalized slavery."

The *bracero* program quickly became operational because Mexicans needed the work and the growers needed labor. Four thousand Mexican workers soon entered the United States; 53,000 came in 1943; and 62,000 arrived in 1944. Between 1942 and 1947, 219,000 Mexicans worked in the fields, half of them in California. When the FSA complained that the growers held wages too low and failed to provide adequate housing, these farmers succeeded in having the program transferred to the War Food Administration, which proved more sympathetic to their needs.

The *braceros* provided essential agricultural labor, but the agreement between the United States and Mexico authorized the termination of this contract labor when the war ended. The growers, however, had become so dependent on this cheap labor that they successfully sought extension of the program. In 1956 some 445,000 *braceros* entered the United States, most of them for work in California and Texas. By 1959 the growers had used the *bracero* program to depress farm wages in California to 47 percent of the national average for manufacturing wages. The program also drove domestic workers from the fields, and the growers used it to undermine efforts to improve working conditions and to break strikes by other agricultural workers. The growers continued to depend on the federal government for the provision of cheap Mexican labor until the civil rights movement brought an end to this abusive agricultural program in 1964. During its twenty-two-year existence, the growers had used it to enormous benefit. Through the *bracero* program, the federal government enabled growers to hold their labor costs to a minimum and prevent reforms for agricultural workers, either domestic or foreign, at the expense of equity and decency. The growers did not willingly give up this dependence on the federal government for the support of their labor needs.

Farmers also relied on the federal government to provide prisoners of war for agricultural labor. Between 1943 and 1946, 155 prisoner-of-war camps and a number of "branch" camps were established across the country. In 1943 the Department of Agriculture, the War Department, and the War Manpower Commission developed a program to supply POWs to farmers who needed agricultural labor. Farmers applied for POW labor through their local extension office. The county agent then notified the nearest camp commander of their need. POWs worked in the sugar beet, cotton, and hay fields, and picked vegetables, dug potatoes, and shocked grain. Farmers paid the federal government the local wage for the work, from which the prisoners received eighty cents per day. POW agricultural labor proved essential and prevented serious loss from a lack of harvest workers. While the war lasted, many farmers came to depend on POW workers—and thereby the federal government—for helping them solve their labor problems.

POSTWAR PROBLEMS

When the war ended, European demands for American agricultural commodities kept prices high, and many farmers attempted to increase prices still more by refusing to market their commodities. As a result, the federal government raised ceiling prices thirty cents per bushel of wheat and fifteen cents per bushel of corn to encourage, or bribe, farmers to sell their grain. The Truman administration also removed price controls on beef to encourage cattlemen to market their livestock. Farmers as well as consumers now opposed price controls. Consumers wanted price controls to end in hope that grocery bills would decline; farmers believed that price controls prevented them from earning more money.

Although the Steagall amendment guaranteed prices at 90 percent of parity for major crops through the 1948 crop year, by the late 1940s farmers had the capacity to produce commodities that far exceeded demand. The federal government and the major farm organizations now began to wrestle with ideas for regulating production while maintaining prices. No one had quick or easy answers to solve the farm problem, but through the 1960s farm policy occupied as much time in Congress as any domestic policy issue. A coherent farm policy that would balance production with demand while maintaining acceptable prices became increasingly difficult because farmers had too many conflicting interests. Cotton farmers, for example, wanted high price supports and strict acreage limitations while Midwestern farmers feared that Southern lands taken out of cotton would be converted to corn produc-

tion. Western cattlemen feared that cropland taken out of production would be converted to grass for grazing purposes, to
their detriment. At the same time high price supports encouraged farmers to produce more of specific commodities than
were needed. Price supports kept commodity and food prices
relatively high, discouraged diversification, and burdened taxpayers and the federal treasury. Farmers, however, did not
wish to return to the days of market-determined prices and
production.

By the autumn of 1948, agricultural policy had become an
important part of the presidential campaign. With farm prices
averaging 110 percent of parity, Harry Truman reminded
farmers in the Midwest that "in 1932, under the Republicans,
we had . . . 15-cent corn and 3-cent hogs." Truman intended to
arouse fears among farmers of serious economic consequences
if the Republicans won the presidential election. He used his
"give 'em hell" campaign style to put the Republican party on
the defensive and to tell voters, particularly in the Midwestern
farm states where his support had ebbed, that Republicans had
"stuck a pitchfork in the farmer's back." The president suggested they would ruin the farm prosperity that the Democrats had initiated in 1933 with the Agricultural Adjustment
Act. Certainly Truman's charges that Republicans would jeop-
ardize farm prosperity was no more accurate than his claims
that the New Deal was responsible for agricultural prosperity.
Yet many farmers believed their best chance to maintain high,
stable commodity prices depended on Truman and the Democratic party.

The farmer needed a "fair deal," Truman declared, but the
danger was that "he may be voted out of a fair deal, and into a
Republican deal." But Republicans also pledged to support the
family farm, agricultural credit, cooperatives, and soil conservation, and even the Democrats called for "a permanent system of flexible [rather than fixed] price supports for

agricultural products, to maintain farm income on a parity with farm operating costs." Republican presidential candidate Thomas E. Dewey, however, spoke little about agricultural policy during the campaign except to charge that the Democrats were intentionally misleading farmers. Perhaps so, but the strategy worked. Several days before the election, Truman told an audience that "any farmer in these United States who votes against his own interests, that is who votes the Republican ticket, ought to have his head examined." By election day, many farmers feared a new farm depression if the Republicans won, because they would end price-support programs.

The Midwestern farm vote helped Truman to victory in the presidential election. While an analysis of the 1948 campaign involves many considerations, many Republican leaders, including Dewey, attributed their defeat to mishandling the farm vote. Many farmers also interpreted the Democratic victory as an endorsement of mandatory price supports at 90 to 100 percent of parity, even though Truman himself favored flexible price supports. Above all, both parties now clearly understood that farmers demanded certain guarantees from the federal government.

Even so, Congress attempted to respond to consumer complaints that commodity price supports increased their cost of living. It did so in 1949 by reducing price supports to between 60 and 90 percent of parity, based on the production of specific crops. Congress also changed the parity formula to make price-supported commodities dependent on the relationship between farm and nonfarm prices during the most recent ten-year period. Larger wheat crops in a given year, for example, would receive a lower price support than smaller crops, but the price of basic crops would be supported at a fixed 90 percent of parity until January 1, 1950. Thus high wartime price supports would continue for another two years, much to the pleasure of farmers across the nation. Thereafter flexible price supports would theoretically encourage farmers to reduce production of commodities whose price declined because of surplus production, and shift to crops that paid higher price supports. But farmers responded to low prices by producing more to make up for their lost income with greater volume.

At the same time many farmers wanted continued high price supports for staple commodities that remained in surplus. The federal government continued to acquire more commodities through the Commodity Credit Corporation to keep them off the market, thereby increasing the cost of the farm program for taxpayers. The former chairman of the House Agriculture Committee, Clifford R. Hope of Kansas, astutely observed that the government's role in agriculture was no longer a matter of debate. Rather, "the principal question with most farmers is not whether they are entitled to 90 percent of parity, but the method to be used in giving it to them."

In 1949 Secretary of Agriculture Charles F. Brannan recommended a major change in agricultural policy. Brannan believed that "the prosperity of our agricultural producers is closely tied up with the prosperity of our entire country." If farmers prospered they would have disposable income that would benefit manufacturing and industry and everyone who worked outside agriculture. In order to improve farm income, Brannan wanted to replace the old parity index schedule based on 1909–1914 agricultural prices with direct income payments to producers. He called these payments "production payments" and defined them as "a payment to the farmer to go on producing to meet genuine consumer needs, rather than restricting output short of that need." Brannan proposed to abandon the parity method for determining price support levels for agricultural products. He would replace it with an income standard determined by a ten-year moving average beginning with the years 1938–1947. He also advocated limits on federal income-support payments based on farm size, with a maximum of $25,700 to ensure that small-scale farmers received most of the financial aid from the federal government. His plan also obligated farmers to practice soil conservation and to observe predetermined production levels. By this Brannan meant "a volume high enough to benefit most farmers but one which will not encourage the development of extremely large, industrialized farms."

Essentially Brannan's plan would have supported prices at about 100 percent of parity in contrast to the maximum payment of 90 percent of parity provided by the Agricultural Act of 1949. Brannan believed his program would chart a new direction for "production and price adjustment with a definite income objective." By basing agricultural policy on income rather than price-support criteria, he contended that the federal government could provide "a realistic minimum below which it is not in the interest of farmers or consumers to allow farm prices to fall." More commodities would also be supported.

Brannan's plan permitted commodity prices to be set by the marketplace. Prices for basic "storable" commodities would continue to be supported by loans, purchase agreements, and direct purchases, but perishable commodities would be supported by income payments. In order to ensure that parity prices would guarantee parity income, for example, the government would pay farmers the difference between the market price and the parity or target price. This payment would be a direct subsidy for production. If, for example, wheat brought two dollars per bushel on the market and the parity price was three dollars per bushel, the farmer would receive a check from the government that paid him one dollar for every bushel of wheat he sold. Brannan believed this agricultural policy would keep staple agricultural commodities abundant, food prices low, and farm income relatively high.

No farm program since the McNary-Haugen plan gener-

ated more controversy than the Brannan plan. It made agricultural policy a major issue in national politics and divided
the farm community. Critics charged that the plan would be
too expensive and a "very high price to pay for a guaranteed
income." At best it would prove little more than a charity program for farmers. Some cotton and wheat farmers, however,
objected because the plan would restrict the amount of money
they could receive from the federal government. One Kansas
wheat farmer wrote to Secretary Brannan in support: "We
want security on the farm, even if we have to control production and have less freedom." Livestock producers, on the other
hand, believed the Brannan plan would increase feed-grain
prices.

The Farmers' Union supported the Brannan plan, but the
American Farm Bureau Federation staunchly opposed it. The
Farm Bureau objected to the plan because it enlarged federal
regulation of the agricultural economy, but more important
because Brannan had not asked the advice of the major farm
organizations. Moreover Farm Bureau members, who tended
to be larger and more prosperous farmers, would have their
federal subsidies restricted by the plan. The "old liberalism" of
New Deal farm policy had become the "new conservatism."
Most farmers preferred the old methods of supporting farm
prices—government loans, direct cash purchases, and allotment and marketing agreements, not direct cash subsidies that
smacked of welfare.

In the end, the Farm Bureau, the Grange, and the National
Council of Farmer Cooperatives mustered enough votes in
Congress to kill the Brannan plan. The Agricultural Act of
1949 continued the policy of fixed price supports at 90 percent
of parity for staple crops, dairy products, hogs, chickens, and
eggs for two more years while providing for flexible price supports from 60 to 90 percent of parity through 1954. Acreage allotments remained, and the parity formula was revised to

include calculations for wages for hired farm labor and wartime commodity payments, which meant higher parity prices.

By the early 1950s agricultural production remained high and the federal government had accumulated large quantities of wheat, corn, cotton, dairy products, and other commodities through the Commodity Credit Corporation. When market prices fell below government loan rates, farmers turned their commodities over to the federal government rather than pay their loan debts. At the same time farmers attempted to make up for lost income from falling prices by producing still more, thereby aggravating the surplus problem. No one seemed capable of solving the problem of surplus production and high government expenditures for price-supporting loans. The principles of the Agricultural Adjustment Act of 1938, as amended by the Agricultural Act of 1949, remained the foundation of American farm policy.*

The Korean War, which began in June 1950, temporarily solved the problem of surplus production and low prices. As demand for agricultural commodities increased, farm prices rose sharply. Commodity prices advanced above parity, and the Commodity Credit Corporation disposed of surpluses stored in government warehouses and elevators. In 1952 Congress protected high wartime prices by amending the Agricultural Act of 1949 to extend price supports on the basic commodities of wheat, cotton, corn, rice, tobacco, and peanuts at a fixed rate of 90 percent of parity through the 1954 crop year. This policy stimulated farmers to expand production.

During the 1952 presidential campaign, Dwight Eisen-

---

*The Agricultural Act of 1949 had no expiration date. Although amended over the years, it remained, along with the Agricultural Adjustment Act of 1938, the basic authority for government price supports until 1996. Neither has been repealed.

hower told farmers that he supported 90 percent parity prices through 1954, and farmers played an important role in sending him to the White House. Once inaugurated, however, Eisenhower and his secretary of agriculture, Ezra Taft Benson, advocated flexible price supports. They argued that high, fixed price supports at 90 percent of parity were simply costing the government too much money. Fixed price supports also encouraged farmers to continue producing commodities already in surplus, rather than diversify by planting more profitable crops, because government price-supporting loans guaranteed them an income. As a result, large surpluses of cotton, wheat, and dairy products held by the Commodity Credit Corporation depressed prices and cost millions of dollars for storage. In 1953 and 1954 alone the CCC acquired $1.5 billion in agricultural commodities. Secretary Benson maintained that the agricultural program inherited by the Eisenhower administration "makes the government the principal owner of a farm commodity." The market, he said, should determine agricultural prices; price supports should serve only as "insurance against disaster."

Eisenhower believed the "farm problem" could be solved by a flexible price-support program that would encourage farmers to shift to commodities with higher price supports, and by supporting increased consumption through school lunch and export programs. The fixed parity price supports of 90 percent of parity would end. But Farm Bloc congressmen believed Eisenhower's proposed policy changes were "politically poisonous," and they had no intention of supporting him. The leading farm organizations rejected the idea of agricultural prices determined by a free-market economy. They demanded federal price-supporting loans at levels that guaranteed a profit and a standard of living for farmers comparable to that of city dwellers. They believed that farm men and women could remain on the land only with government support.

Commercial farmers preferred this guaranteed income rather than cast their fate to the competitive, free-market world economy that always threatened to return lower income. Although the Farm Bureau favored flexible price supports and the Farmers' Union advocated high, fixed price supports, these major farm organizations differed only in degree—neither wanted the federal government to lower price supports below profitable levels.

Eisenhower discovered that sensible agricultural economics and sensible farm politics were difficult to reconcile, but he achieved a compromise flexible price-support program. In 1954 Congress approved the Agricultural Trade Development and Assistance Act. Known as Public Law 480, or the "Food for Peace" program, this legislation authorized the federal government to dispose of agricultural surpluses abroad, particularly to help friendly, needy, and underdeveloped nations. Even so, the new legislation still provided for the federal subsidization of agricultural prices that ranged from 82.5 to 90 percent of parity and thereby guaranteed farm income. Although critics of farm policy accused farmers of being on the dole, continued surplus production forced agricultural prices down while farm expenses increased. By the mid-1950s per capita disposable income on the farm averaged only 48 percent of that of the nonagricultural population, down from 58 percent at the turn of the decade. As long as farmers could not control production or set prices, they could only depend on government price supports to keep them economically viable. Many farm programs, such as the support given burley tobacco farmers, kept small-scale farmers on the land and slowed consolidation. Even so, many men and women continued to leave the farms for better jobs and a higher standard of living in the towns and cities.

While consumers and farmers complained about high food prices and government policy, Secretary Benson grumbled that a "technological explosion" on the farm ensured overproduction and low commodity prices. In an effort to combat the problem, the Eisenhower administration looked to the past and proposed a new plan to limit production. Introduced as the Agricultural Act of 1956, and informally known as the Soil Bank Program, this legislation authorized the federal government to pay farmers a fixed amount per acre for removing cotton, corn, wheat, peanut, rice, and tobacco lands from production. Farmers could not use these acres for any form of agricultural production. Rather, the lands were designated a conservation reserve for a maximum of ten years. Weeds would grow and help conserve the soil. With fewer acres in production, surpluses would diminish and agricultural prices would rise. Farmers would receive federal payments for reducing their allotted acreage of certain crops if they used those acres for conservation purposes. Theoretically market prices would increase as farmers reduced production. Farmers and congressmen from the agricultural states liked the idea of being paid for removing land from production, but they did not wish to move toward prices determined by a free-market economy.

Secretary Benson hoped the Soil Bank Program would encourage many small-scale farmers to take all their lands out of production and leave agriculture altogether, thereby helping solve what the USDA perceived as the problem of too many farmers producing too many crop surpluses. Farmers, however, were divided over the potential of the Soil Bank Program to solve the farm problem. Although many of them participated in the program and received payments for withdrawing 28 million acres from production, they withdrew only the least productive lands. Consequently the Soil Bank Program did little to reduce surpluses. While the Grange favored a commodity-by-commodity approach to prices and production, the Farm Bureau hailed the Soil Bank Program as the "best farm program to date for production adjustment." Soon, however, many farmers realized that the program would not solve the cost-price squeeze. After payments under the program severely taxed the federal treasury, the government abandoned it in 1959.

While farmers across the nation participated in the Soil Bank Program, others in the Great Plains looked to the federal government for more aid in the 1950s when drought returned to the region. In the old Dust Bowl farmers suffered severe wind erosion, and the federal government quickly provided $15 million, with more to come, to help them meet emergency conservation expenses, such as plowing and strip cropping. Cattlemen also sought long-term loans at low interest rates and low-cost feed subsidized by the federal government. In 1953 T. L. Roach, president of the Texas and Southwestern Cattle Raisers Association, told the chairman of the House Agriculture Committee, "Cattlemen justifiably feel that the government should immediately do something to help them survive." He urged the government to sell cotton-seed cake, corn, and other feed grains at reduced rates from its reserves and to grant credit at low interest rates for those purchases. This aid seemed only fair to the cattlemen, and "if the government intend[ed] continuing the use of food items for foreign-relief programs, it could arrange to buy and can cattle, especially cows from the disaster area, and use this canned meat in such relief programs." Shading its real motives for beef price supports under the cloak of patriotism, the Oklahoma Cattlemen's Association recommended that government canned beef be distributed through the Office of Civil Defense "to guard against food shortage in the case of national emergency or disaster due to atomic attack." The Farmers Home Administration, which supervised most drought-relief programs, also provided loans to cattlemen to purchase feed and hay and to farmers to buy seed, fertilizer, and equipment necessary to remain on the land until the drought ended and normal production returned.

SCIENCE AND TECHNOLOGY

While farmers took advantage of government price supports, loans, and conservation programs, they looked to science and technology to help increase productivity and offset income losses from postwar price declines. By late 1945 farmers were eagerly buying new twine binders, self-propelled combines, corn pickers, and tractors despite their scarcity and high prices. The growth in tractors corresponded with fewer numbers of horses needed for draft; acreage heretofore used for forage could be shifted to crops for human consumption. As a result, nearly 2.5 million acres were freed for other agricultural purposes by the end of 1945. The mechanical cotton picker also became the most important technological development on a regional level. First marketed in 1942 by the International Harvester Company, large-scale cotton producers in the South and West began to adopt this machine in the 1950s. By the early 1960s mechanical cotton pickers harvested 72 percent of the crop.

In the months that followed the end of World War II, farmers also increasingly adopted electrification. In 1940, 35 percent of all farms had electricity. By 1945 nearly half of all farms had electric power, and electricity became a "utility" rather than a "luxury" on farms across the country. It no longer powered only conveniences such as vacuum cleaners, refrigerators, and lightbulbs. Now it helped boost profits from the dairy barn to the feedlot to the henhouse by powering milk coolers, feed grinders, and heating systems. By 1960 almost 98 percent of all farmers enjoyed electric service.

In other scientific changes after the war, farmers began

using heavy applications of chemical fertilizer to ameliorate the problem of soil depletion, caused in part by extensive wartime production. They also began applying newly developed insecticides, such as DDT. Farmers hailed it as a "miracle worker" and a "cure-all" for insect control. Certainly DDT turned out to be the "atom bomb" of insecticides, capable of killing flies, mosquitoes, fleas, Colorado potato beetles, Japanese beetles, leafhoppers, and many other insects. Allegedly it was "neither poisonous to the animals nor irritating to the operator." By 1947 an estimated 95 percent of commercial fruit growers used DDT. During the late 1940s farmers also began using the pre-emergent herbicide 2, 4-D in their cornfields. In sugar beet fields alone, the petrochemical industry estimated that chemical weed killers cost growers only $5 per acre compared with cultivation costs of $40 per acre for hand labor. Chemical technology seemed a heaven-sent blessing. Although some people questioned the effects of chemical pesticides and herbicides on public health, most farmers believed the postwar chemical industry had ushered in a "golden age."

AGRIBUSINESS

In the 1950s most agricultural economists and government officials believed that too many farmers remained on the land. They considered small-scale, marginal farmers a nuisance if not a hindrance to the consolidation of farms and improved efficiency through high capitalization. By using expensive technology to increase production and reduce costs, farmers could put more profit into their bank accounts.

Confronted with high operating costs, many farmers chose to give up considerable freedom of action by contracting with agricultural corporations to produce specific commodities for a guaranteed price. Although some fruit and vegetable farmers had practiced contract farming for some time, by the mid-

1950s more farmers were choosing this form of operation to reduce their financial risk. In contract farming, a company such as Campbell Soup, Ralston Purina, or Sunkist Growers contracts with a farmer to produce a certain amount of tomatoes, chickens, or oranges for a specific price. (In the case of chickens, the company provides the chicks, feed, and other supplies. In return, the farmer agrees to raise a certain number of chickens by a specific time, for which the company pays him for his labor. The company makes the essential decisions for the farmer, such as the mix and amount of grain to feed the chickens.) As a result, the farmer receives a guaranteed income. Contract farming also removes a farmer's worries about credit, interest rates, and low prices. But contract farmers in effect work for a company, not for themselves.

Contract farming is known as "vertical integration" because the agricultural company involved with the farmer controls the commodity from production on the farm to its processing and marketing to the consumer. In 1955 John H. Davis, a former assistant secretary of agriculture, used the term *agribusiness*—by which he meant "the sum total of all operations involved in the production and distribution of food and fiber"—to define vertical integration and the business of agriculture. In this broad sense, agribusiness means more than the relationship between food conglomerates and farmers. Cooperatives such as Sunkist Growers and others, which operate retail outlets for farmers and sell everything from gasoline to groceries, are also components of agribusiness in the United States. These cooperatives seek to consolidate services and integrate all the production of their members into their business activities.

As farm men and women came to depend on the federal government or contract farming to maintain their way of life, they raised a fundamental question that would remain unanswered for the rest of the twentieth century: Is there a moral obligation to save the family farm? In 1960 Congress passed the Family Income Act, which declared that the federal government supported "the family system of agriculture against all forms of collectivization . . . in full recognition that the system of independent family farms was the beginning and foundation of free enterprise in America . . . that it holds for the future the greatest promise of security and abundance of food and fiber, and that it is an ever-present source of strength for democratic processes and the American idea." But by 1960, most of the poultry production in the nation, for example, was controlled by feed companies such as Ralston Purina. Few independent, diversified farmers raised chickens. Agribusiness mushroomed over the next decade. Still, myth effectively competed with reality in farm policy.

AGRICULTURAL ORGANIZATIONS

Although farmers wanted government aid during the postwar years, they could not agree on the amount of federal support or the regulations that came with it. The American Farm Bureau Federation continued to advocate flexible price supports to encourage farmers to shift production to more profitable crops while ensuring at least some guaranteed income. Flexible price supports, the Farm Bureau contended, would also loosen government controls, particularly in the form of acreage allotments. The Farm Bureau continued to believe that fixed price supports created surpluses by encouraging farmers to raise price-supported crops. In turn, surpluses drove down market prices. With more than a million members concentrated primarily in the Midwest and South, the Farm Bureau carried considerable influence in Congress. By contrast, the Farmers' Union had relatively few members, with its strength concentrated in the northern Great Plains. It favored high, fixed price supports at 100 percent of parity and government-mandated acreage allotments or reductions. The Grange favored price supports, the amount depending on the specific commodity, rather than blanket, fixed coverage, but it emphasized the traditional social, cultural, and educational features of the organization.

Many farmers believed that none of the major agricultural organizations met their needs. Instead they began to form special commodity organizations, such as the National Association of Wheat Growers and the National Milk Producers Federation, which joined the American Cotton Association, among others, to seek government aid for their memberships alone. Moreover, as political power continued to shift from rural to urban areas, farm groups believed the federal government gave them less attention than they deserved. This feeling of powerlessness, or at least the government's slighting of their interests, led to the founding of the most radical farm organization in the postwar era.

In 1955 a small group of radical farmers in the Midwest formed the National Farmers' Organization (NFO). This group used the Farmers' Holiday Association as its model for dramatic action to force the federal government to meet its demands. Although the NFO was a comparatively small organization, its members sought economic relief through collective action. The NFO intended to negotiate contracts with commodity buyers that would guarantee cost-of-production prices and a profit. If buyers, such as food processors, refused to sign contracts that provided these prices, the NFO proposed a farm strike—called a "holding action"—that would last until buyers met their demands. By the end of the decade the NFO was struggling for recognition and legitimacy and fighting to become a major player in the formulation of federal agricultural policy. NFO members were becoming impatient and talked about "direct action" to force the federal government and commodity buyers to meet their demands.

Overall the most successful lobbyists for federal support during the 1950s were the commodity groups. Congress considered them moderate and reasonable in their demands in contrast to the conservative Farm Bureau, the interventionist Farmers' Union, or the radical National Farmers' Organization.

Between the onset of World War II and the Korean War, the American farmer experienced the longest sustained period of prosperity in American history. Yet while wartime brought high agricultural prices, many problems remained. By May 1949 surplus production, fostered in part by science and technology, caused farm prices to plummet 26 percent while the cost of living dropped only 3.5 percent. Farmers began to feel the cost-price squeeze that would plague them for the remainder of the century. At the same time prices fell, consumers, who outnumbered farmers about five to one, began revolting against high food prices. Many consumers believed that government price supports increased the cost of food. Every plan that promised to solve the complex problem of low prices, surplus production, and government subsidies also threatened to change farm life across the nation fundamentally.

In the late 1940s farmers also became increasingly specialized and mechanized—they relied on one or two crops and more technology. This trend contributed to the continued decline of the farm population and the number of farms. In 1940, 30.5 million farmers comprised the agricultural population who lived on 6.1 million farms that averaged 175 acres. By 1950 the farm population had dropped to 23 million on 5.3 million farms that averaged 216 acres. Between 1940 and 1950, as farm men and women left the countryside for better jobs and a higher standard of living in urban areas, the farm population declined from 23.2 percent to 15.3 percent of the total population.

Farmers increased production by 2.1 percent each year in the 1950s despite government programs designed to limit production. At the same time the population increased approximately 1.7 percent annually, and per capita food consumption remained relatively constant. Exports also failed to remove enough surplus agricultural commodities to raise prices. By 1960 the federal government was paying $7.7 billion to acquire surplus agricultural products through the Commodity Credit Corporation in order to keep those commodities off the market and thereby prevent prices from declining still further while providing needed income for farmers.

Although no other nation could compete with American farmers in terms of productivity, diversity, and wealth, government attempts to reduce surplus production and increase market prices were defeated by technology and science. And while commodity prices remained low, the cost of operating a farm rose. Those farmers who could afford to purchase more acreage needed to invest in more technology, particularly tractors, combines, and corn and cotton pickers, in order to expand production to offset low prices and high capital investment.

While production remained high, prices were insufficient to enable many farmers to maintain full-time operations. More and more farmers sought off-farm employment to make ends meet. Since many farmers were "long on labor and short on land," they necessarily worked away from the farm to support their families. Good roads and better opportunities to make money off the farm enabled them to gain additional income to pay debts and make improvements. Farm women too began taking outside jobs in the 1950s, in part because home conveniences saved time, but more often because their families needed the income. In the mid-1950s more than 630,000 farmers worked away from their land for 100 days or more each year. By 1960 part-time farming no longer represented a period during which farmers worked in outside employment to build capital to begin full-time farming. At the same time off-farm employment required farmers to make adjustments, such as changing from time-intensive dairying to beef production.

In spite of the need to seek off-farm employment, many farmers remained on the land because they believed in the "values of rural living." The family farm, like the church, the local school, and the Supreme Court, remained a symbol of freedom and democracy, and farmers strongly defended it. But by 1960 farming had become more than a way of life; it was a business where only the most efficient survived. The days of the small-scale, diversified farmer were gone. Government policy in the form of loans, price supports, and acreage reductions favored large-scale farmers who could produce more for less cost than small-scale landowners. As a result, farmers became increasingly dependent on the federal government for their standard of living.

By 1960 the farm population and the number of farms continued to decline. Only 15.6 million people remained on 3.9 million farms. Farm men and women now composed only 8.7 percent of the total population, down from 23.2 percent in 1940. Despite the decline in the farm population, farmers became more productive than ever before, and the size of the average farm increased from 175 to about 300 acres. Clearly, small-scale farmers were being replaced by larger, more efficient operators.

Yet farm income remained below that of city dwellers, averaging only $1,083 compared with $2,014 for nonfarmers. In 1960 farmers had only about 54 percent of the purchasing power of nonfarmers. High operating costs also continued to erode farmers' earnings.

Some urban critics of farm policy argued that price supports increased food costs. Others contended that the $4 billion expenditure by the Commodity Credit Corporation to acquire wheat, corn, and cotton, and more than $1 million per day in storage costs, placed an undue burden on taxpayers. Still other critics charged that farmers lived comfortable lives on federal handouts. According to one critic, "It took farmers a long time to pry open the doors of the federal treasury, but since they succeeded the bounty has been unceasing."

Farmers, of course, disagreed. They argued that their operating costs exceeded their income, and they continued to leave the land and seek employment elsewhere. Those who stayed on the land continued to look to the federal government for aid, and neither Congress nor the USDA disappointed them.

5

Fallout

BETWEEN World War II and the mid-1990s, American agriculture changed dramatically. In the South, farmers began specializing in high-value crops and livestock. Although they continued to raise the traditional crops of cotton, tobacco, rice, sugarcane, and peanuts, cotton dropped from its pedestal as king. Soybeans, hay, beef cattle, and poultry now became major agricultural activities. Southern agriculture diversified, not for subsistence but for commercial production. By the late 1970s landowners rather than tenants operated most Southern farms. African-American farmers had essentially vanished from the land; by the late 1980s only about 23,000 remained. Agriculture in the South became more like farming in other regions. It lost much of its distinctiveness as Southern farmers shifted their emphasis to matters of capitalization, mechanization, and labor efficiency.

In the North, dairying for the production and marketing of fluid milk to urban consumers remained a major agricultural activity. Across the Midwest, farmers specialized in the production of corn, soybeans, hogs, and poultry. Increasingly hog and poultry producers signed contracts with processors in order to reduce their risk, acquire necessary capital, and earn a guaranteed profit. Many Midwestern farmers, led by the Farm Bureau, advocated less government in agriculture, expanded markets, and the development of new industrial products from agricultural commodities that would increase prices and improve their income. At the same time they wanted to retain government price supports.

In the West, farmers on the Great Plains emphasized the production of wheat, cattle, cotton, and soybeans. Absentee ownership and tenancy remained high. Farm size and technology became critical determinants for success or failure in the absence of bad weather or glutted domestic and international markets. Farmers in California became major producers of rice and, along with Arizona, cotton, while wheat farming prevailed on the eastern plains of Washington. California, however, epitomized Western agriculture with its fruit and vegetable production, usually with hired migrant labor.

The Policy of Dependency

No presidential candidate knew less about agriculture than John Kennedy, but during the 1960 campaign his relative ignorance did not prevent him from declaring that "the family farm should remain the backbone of American agriculture. We must take positive action to promote and strengthen this form of farm enterprise." Throughout his campaign Kennedy pleased farmers by pointing out that "the decline in agricultural income is the number one domestic problem in the United States." He pledged to help relieve the farmers' cost-price squeeze with a new program that relied on the concept of supply management. Farmers would receive parity income with nonfarmers if they accepted mandatory production or marketing controls.

During the 1960 presidential campaign, the differences between Kennedy and Richard Nixon, the Republican contender, over agricultural policy were clear and important. Kennedy supported production and marketing controls and price guarantees while Nixon opposed them. Nixon considered the problem of farmers' income temporary; Kennedy believed it to be long term. Kennedy contended that the "small but chronic surplus in agriculture" was "depressing prices and incomes"; Nixon thought the agricultural surplus problem could be ended in a few years so that farmers could "operate in free markets with a minimum of [government] aid." During the campaign the Democrats also advocated "full parity income for farmers by balancing production and consumption," which meant acreage reduction and the distribution of commodity surpluses to school lunch programs, the needy, and as foreign aid. Republicans ignored the issue of parity income but pledged to increase farm prices by placing more crop acreage in conservation reserves, expanding foreign markets, and increasing food distribution at home. Nevertheless Democrats and Republicans essentially differed only over the extent of production controls and the level of price supports.

When he came to office, President Kennedy advocated an even greater regulatory state for agriculture. His ideas about supply management—restricting production and marketing, including marketing quotas, to maintain high agricultural prices—had their origins in New Deal agricultural policy, particularly the Agricultural Adjustment Act of 1938 as amended by the Agricultural Act of 1949. Under Kennedy's supply management policy, market prices would increase above support price levels by reducing the quantities of commodities marketed instead of reducing surplus through acreage reduction programs. Kennedy reasoned that farmers would not have an incentive to increase production by using more fertilizer or other forms of science and technology if quotas regulated commodity sales. Thus under Kennedy's program farmers would receive higher price supports if they limited the amount of commodities they sold. Ultimately Kennedy hoped to reduce federal expenditures for agriculture, but this goal required a long-term commitment to balancing production with world food needs. It also demanded production and marketing controls that would limit agricultural commodities in storage and trade as well as guarantee parity income. Kennedy believed that strict marketing controls were necessary to ensure that farmers received parity income and a return on their investment comparable with nonfarmers.

Marketing control, then, was essential to supply management, and farmers who participated in the program would necessarily relinquish some control over production decisions. Kennedy did not consider this loss of freedom by farmers a sacrifice. He contended that "men agree among themselves to limit their unrestricted 'freedom' in some field in order to achieve some other goal that is highly valued." Such action, he argued, was "the act of rational and civilized man." Kennedy told farmers that his program "gives you no assurances that you can have high incomes *and* unlimited production and no controls," but "we pledge ourselves to securing full parity income . . . which gives average producers a return on their invested capital, labor, and management equal to that which similar, or comparable, resources earn in non-farm employment." But, he cautioned, "a basic instrument of assuring parity of income will be supply management controls—including marketing quotas, land retirement . . . and other devices."

When Kennedy assumed the presidency, corn and wheat prices had fallen to postwar lows while their surpluses had reached record highs. The Kennedy administration quickly responded when Secretary of Agriculture Orville Freeman and USDA advisers drafted legislation known as the "emergency" Feed Grain Bill. Designed to help reduce surplus feed grains, particularly corn, to improve farm income, and to reduce government expenses, the Feed Grain Program enabled farmers to divert between 20 and 40 percent of their acreage, depending on farm size, from the production of corn, barley,

and sorghum. Farmers who reduced their acreage by 20 percent and shifted it into a conservation program were guaranteed an income of 60 percent of the gross value of the normal
production from that acreage. If they reduced their acreage an
additional 20 percent, they would receive greater payments.
Farmers who chose not to participate in the crop-reduction
program could produce as much as they pleased, but they
would be at the mercy of market prices. The federal government intended to dump feed grains on the market periodically
to keep prices low and encourage—if not force—farmers to
participate in the Feed Grain Program. This program aimed
to control production rather than marketing.

Despite a reduction of 26 million acres of corn in 1961,
farmers harvested only 11 percent less than they had the previous year—more than the administration's targeted reduction of 18 percent. Farmers increased the application of
fertilizer and diverted their poorest lands. Nevertheless the
Feed Grain Program played a major role in boosting farm
income by $1 billion, primarily by selling more bushels at
government-guaranteed prices to the Commodity Credit Corporation. Some farmers who did not participate in this crop-
reduction program also expanded production in order to take
advantage of possible higher prices from lower production nationwide.

Dairy farmers and livestock producers were reluctant to
participate because they were interested in cheap feed grains.
A smaller feed grain crop promised only to increase their operating costs. Nevertheless farmers who participated in the
Feed Grain Program liked it because the program was voluntary rather than mandatory, and because those who participated received a guaranteed income. Congress extended the
program into 1962.

Cotton farmers, however, opposed mandatory acreage restrictions to reduce production and increase prices. Instead

they favored maximum production with government export subsidies to help cover losses due to low world market prices. The Kennedy administration wanted the votes of Southern Democrats and provided an export subsidy so that cotton farmers could sell on the world market and still make a profit.

Kennedy also knew that city dwellers would not support government programs that raised food prices. In order to reduce agricultural surpluses and increase agricultural prices, which would relieve taxpayers from supporting expensive farm programs, Kennedy began reducing government-owned commodities by reinstituting the food stamp program and by expanding school lunch and milk programs. His administration also expanded the Food for Peace program. Still, mandatory acreage and marketing regulations were necessary to adjust supply to demand.

In 1962 Kennedy sent to Congress the Food and Agriculture Bill. Upon approval it provided for mandatory acreage and marketing controls in return for a guarantee of 90 percent parity prices if two-thirds of participating farmers agreed. Surprisingly, in 1963 wheat farmers voted to reject those controls and accept 50 percent parity prices. Based on current wheat prices, producers believed they could make more money with unrestricted production and a guaranteed price of $1.25 per bushel rather than restricted production and a price guarantee of approximately $2.00 per bushel. Wheat farmers evidently also voted to reject mandatory controls based on the argument of the Farm Bureau, which contended that mandatory controls would lead to restrictions on other commodities. In addition, many small-scale farmers who voted on the referendum did not raise wheat as a primary crop. These farmers had fewer acres to take out of production, and they wanted to produce as much as possible no matter the price so long as the government guaranteed them 50 percent of parity prices. In reality, however, wheat farmers wanted more, not less, from the federal government. They no doubt understood that the government might provide an even better financial program without mandatory controls if they rejected the plan to restrict wheat production and marketing.

Before President Kennedy's assassination in November 1963, his administration achieved some success in administering a voluntary rather than a mandatory control program to restrict production and increase prices for farmers who produced feed grains. But the Kennedy administration never solved the problems of overproduction, low farm income, and the continued decline of the agricultural population. Essentially political partisanship and division among the farm organizations prevented Kennedy from devising a farm program that would substantially reduce surpluses, boost income, and keep farmers on the land. While most farmers wanted federal aid, they opposed government programs that required or mandated production controls. Rather, they supported voluntary production controls provided they could accept government price and income supports without sacrificing much production.

The division of farmers over Kennedy's Feed Grain Program indicated the basic problem facing the American farmer. No single group represented their diverse needs. Some farmers preferred price supports linked to acreage or marketing controls. Others favored the expansion of export markets. The interests of the cash grain farmers were not those of dairymen or livestock producers. Thus farmers remained divided over the solution to the farm problem. Essentially they all agreed that supply had to be brought into balance with demand, and most believed that government policy had to be fashioned to achieve that balance while keeping prices at an acceptable level to preserve the family farm. As a group, however, farmers did not believe that policies based on marketing quotas or land-diversion programs were in their best interests. Some farmers favored a free market and argued that net farm income would increase if the federal government would terminate all farm programs. They held this belief despite economic studies indicating that a free market would cause agricultural prices to fall as much as 40 percent.

During the 1964 presidential campaign, Democratic candidate Lyndon Johnson did not have serious agricultural problems to address. Foreign sales due to the relaxation of trade barriers with Communist countries had diminished government-owned wheat and feed grains. Johnson did not deliver a major agricultural policy address during his entire campaign. Republican candidate Barry Goldwater also essentially ignored farm policy. Once elected, Johnson and a Democratic Congress abandoned the idea of mandatory controls and supported the expansion of markets and voluntary production controls to provide acceptable commodity prices. The result was the Food and Agriculture Act of 1965, which provided direct income payments via price supports for wheat, cotton, feed grains, and other major crops through 1970 to farmers who agreed to participate in existing acreage-reduction programs.

Essentially, then, during the 1960s farm policy remained tied to the ideas developed during the 1930s to control production, shrink surpluses, and increase prices and income. Although most farmers opposed mandatory production and marketing controls, they favored government aid in the form of price supports for voluntary acreage reduction on specific crops to ensure an income floor. Given increased operating costs and farmers' inability to organize and bargain collectively, they remained dependent on the federal government. Without base price supports, the exodus from the farm would have been even greater. Farmers continued to use government to protect their interests.

During the 1968 presidential campaign, Republican

Richard Nixon and Democrat Hubert Humphrey both supported farm programs that would maintain acceptable agricultural prices. With per capita farm income averaging about
75 percent of nonfarm per capita income—up from about 50
percent a decade earlier—the most serious agricultural concerns came from city dwellers who complained about high
taxes to pay for expensive farm programs. Congress ignored
those concerns in passing the Agriculture Act of 1970, which
ensured price supports and gave farmers more freedom to
produce. But Congress limited payments on a single crop to
$50,000 annually. Some observers believed this limit reflected
the declining political power of the Farm Bloc, but it did not
involve significant financial hardship for any group. South
Dakota Senator George McGovern called the action "consis-
tent with the policy of encouraging family farm agriculture."
In fact this legislation reflected the continued power of agriculture in Congress, where Southerners and Midwesterners
dominated the House and Senate agriculture committees despite the shift in voting power from rural to urban areas. Indeed, farmers remained one of the most powerful groups in
American politics because farm-state congressmen often
joined with their urban counterparts to gain support for agricultural programs in return for the backing of urban programs.

In 1971 Congress reflected the continuing political power of
agriculture by providing $8.1 billion to the U.S. Department
of Agriculture, an increase from the $7.7 billion that the
Nixon administration had requested and the largest single annual appropriation for the department to that time. Earl Butz,
the new secretary of agriculture, urged farmers to plant "from
fencerow to fencerow" to take advantage of favorable economic conditions. The farm problem seemed less serious now,
with exports remaining high into mid-decade. Thanks to

Soviet purchases, surpluses declined and market prices rose above target prices.

The Agriculture and Consumer Protection Act of 1973, however, reintroduced the concept of "target prices" from the old Brannan plan. If the market price dropped below Commodity Credit Corporation loan levels, the federal government would make up the difference in a "deficiency payment." For example, if the target price for wheat was $2.50 per bushel, but the market price reached only $1.50, the government would pay participating farmers $1.00 per bushel as a deficiency payment to prop up farm income provided they agreed to specific acreage allotments for production.

Inflation caused by the Vietnam War brought increased food prices. Consumers complained so vociferously that, in 1973, President Gerald Ford placed an embargo on exports of soybeans and cottonseed to reduce feed costs for livestock and poultry producers. The government also froze beef prices. That policy angered farmers and livestock producers. They felt betrayed by a government that had urged them to expand production but that now denied them the benefits of their labor. In July 1975 they became even more upset when longshoremen, angry over food prices, refused to load grain bound for the Soviet Union. Governor Robert Bennett of Kansas declared that "this arrogant action cannot and must not be tolerated by the American people," while William Kuhfuss, president of the American Farm Bureau Federation called the boycott "nothing short of piracy." The Ford embargo and the boycott catapulted agricultural policymaking into the 1976 presidential campaign, in which Democratic candidate Jimmy Carter pledged that he would never embargo agricultural commodities or betray the American farmer.

Once in office, however, Carter proved more sympathetic to consumers than farmers. And increased petroleum costs following the Arab-Israeli War in 1973, together with restricted export markets, placed farmers in an increasingly difficult financial position. Although in 1975 gross farm income rose to $100.5 billion for farmers nationwide, net farm income declined from $34.3 billion in 1973 to $25.5 billion two years later. Many farm enterprises now had greater capital investments than businesses in the towns and cities. The axiom of the decade became "Get bigger, get better, or get out." Unable to control prices or to organize and bargain collectively, farmers believed they had no choice other than to increase production in order to lower unit costs and thereby maintain a profitable business.

More mechanical and chemical technology as well as new farming methods, such as "no till," helped cut costs, conserve soil, reduce labor, and increase production. Many farmers attempted to expand their acreage. The average farm increased from 373 acres in 1970 to 426 acres by the end of the decade. While individual farms got bigger, between 1970 and 1980 their number declined from 2.9 million to 2.4 million. During that time the prices received by farmers dropped sharply while the prices they paid more than doubled. Greater operating costs once again forced farmers to increase productivity in order to meet the cost-price squeeze.

As always, increased production exacerbated the problems of surpluses and low prices. Thus increased efficiency in the long run offered no solution to the farm problem. Contrary to other businesses, farmers were penalized in the marketplace for their efficiency. While they complained about the cost-price squeeze and government policy, some got bigger and better, but thousands fled the farm for the promise of a better life in urban America.

COLLAPSE

Despite record productivity by the early 1980s, partly due to improvements brought about through science and technology and good management practices, old problems remained. Farmers often divided regionally and within commodity groups because their interests were too varied to permit collective action, and surplus production held prices relatively low. Foreign sales boosted prices, but when international agreements were halted or terminated, farmers believed the federal government had betrayed them—even though the Commodity Credit Corporation continued to purchase all their grain at target prices to maintain farm income. The cost-price squeeze continued to erode profits, and farmers remained vulnerable to rapid price increases for fuel, oil, and petroleum-based products. Many farmers tried to prevent financial losses by specializing and becoming more efficient in cash grain production while reducing operating costs. Those who could not afford to do so left the farm, particularly those farmers who had become "paper millionaires" during the 1970s—that is, they had purchased additional acreage with loans. On paper they might own property worth more than a million dollars, but if they could not meet their payments, the lending institution seized their real property.

In the early 1980s agricultural prices continued to fall, primarily due to overproduction, while a strong dollar hurt agricultural sales on the international market. Lower incomes prevented many farmers from meeting their obligations, and lower land values reduced their borrowing power. As a result, many farmers began to experience "extreme" difficulty by the spring of 1986, and their prospects for recovery turned dismal at best. Many farmers experienced "serious" cash-flow problems. More and more farmers were forced to take off-farm employment in order to stay on the land.

Ronald Reagan rode into the presidency intent on cutting federal spending, but Reagan admitted that he did not understand the concept of "parity prices." When he took office, the Food and Agriculture Act of 1977 neared its five-year expiration date, and Congress went to work on a new farm bill. In the resulting Agriculture and Food Act of 1981, Congress tried to meet the needs of each agricultural commodity group within its fixed budget for a farm program. In the past Congress had allowed the commodity groups to negotiate programs with the House and Senate agriculture committees, and the resulting farm budget reflected the combined costs of the benefits provided to the various agricultural groups. In 1981, however, the agriculture committees attempted to fit the requests of each commodity group into a predetermined budget in order to save money and hold farm program costs under control. The ensuing debate proved acrimonious as farm groups bitterly contested for their share of federal aid. The result was the most short-lived farm legislation since 1949. More than 230 groups testified during hearings on the bill. Republicans tried to move agriculture toward a more market-oriented economy with fewer restrictions on planted acreage and the repeal of target prices. Commodity groups demanded a continuation of target price supports.

The debate over a new farm bill produced the Agriculture and Food Act of 1981. Target prices and acreage controls remained. Congress set maximum program payments per individual, except for disaster payments, at $50,000. The legislation also expanded Public Law 480 to help reduce the surplus of government-owned commodities held in warehouses and elevators by the Commodity Credit Corporation. Soon thereafter production boomed, and commodity surpluses increased dramatically while world demand for U.S. agricultural products declined because of foreign competition. Consequently government-held commodities grew enormously and farm program costs spiraled. In addition, operating costs remained high and interest rates skyrocketed, which forced the Reagan administration to increase target price supports and maintain acreage limitations. In 1982 the Department of Agriculture attempted to reduce surplus production and increase commodity prices by requiring wheat, cotton, and rice farmers to reduce their acreage by 10 percent in order to qualify for price supports. This policy had little effect as farmers responded to such regulations as they had in the past: they took their worst lands out of production and increased production on their best lands, often with heavy applications of fertilizer. Government-owned commodity surpluses increased still further.

In 1985 Congress replaced the 1981 farm legislation with the Food Security Act. Although Jesse Helms, a North Carolina Republican and chairman of the Senate Committee on Agriculture, called it a "slow but decisive transition to market-oriented farm policy," it differed little from past farm legislation. Farmers demanded government support, and they got it. The 1985 law used deficiency payments to prop up farm income and retained the nonrecourse loan program through the Commodity Credit Corporation. The act also provided for a long-term land retirement program similar to the Soil Bank Program but now called the Conservation Reserve Program, in which the government paid farmers for taking the land out of production and returning it to grass. The government also worked to expand foreign markets.

The agricultural legislation of the 1980s, however, proved inadequate in solving the collapse of the agricultural economy. Comparatively high agricultural prices and improved foreign markets in the 1970s, and a government policy that had encouraged maximum land use, had increased production. By the early 1980s gross agricultural income had increased to $62 billion. Farmers had used their extra income to invest in new technology and more land. Often, however, they had borrowed money betting that prices would remain high indefinitely. The farm debt that totaled $60 billion in 1972 had skyrocketed to $216 billion in 1983.

As farmers competed for land in the 1970s they bid up prices, but higher land values also gave them more borrowing power. As the national economy also expanded, inflation rates rose substantially, but when the Federal Reserve attempted to slow the rate of inflation in 1979 by raising interest rates to curb spending, restrict credit, and halt inflation, farmers who were deeply in debt found that their production costs also increased. Soon many of them could not meet the payments on their loans, particularly for land and equipment. Banks began to call in their loans, and many farmers who could not pay faced bankruptcy and foreclosure.

Farmers again looked to the federal government for aid. Unlike past times, however, they did not organize effectively to protest their declining economic fortunes, in part because so few farmers remained on the land. In 1985 only 5.3 million people comprised the farm population; only 2.2 percent of the total population were farmers. By the end of the decade, farmers, agricultural organizations, and political supporters could persuade Congress only to make minor changes in farm policy with the Food, Agriculture, Conservation, and Trade Act of 1990. The basic price support, production, and marketing philosophy for farm policy remained little changed since the 1930s.

EMBARGO

While farmers have looked to the federal government for economic support, and while they have participated in a number of programs that have benefited them financially, they have also adamantly opposed government policies that have threatened to limit their exports and profits. On January 4, 1980, President Jimmy Carter imposed an embargo of grain to the Soviet Union to punish the Russians for their invasion of Afghanistan in December 1979. Although Presidents Richard Nixon and Gerald Ford had imposed embargoes on exports of oilseeds and oilseed products to ensure domestic supplies and ease domestic food prices, Carter had pledged during the presidential campaign of 1976 that if elected he would "never again" impose embargoes. As president, however, Carter believed he could use a grain embargo to help force the Russians from Afghanistan. He intended to use food as a tool of foreign policy. Or, as one observer put it, "The U.S. would do with grain what Saudi Arabia had done for oil."

In October 1979 the United States had contracted to sell 25 million tons of wheat and corn to the Soviet Union over the next year. The Soviets quickly completed the purchase of 8 million tons but had not purchased the remaining amount when they invaded Afghanistan. In November, when Iran took a number of American embassy personnel hostage, presidential contenders Senator Edward Kennedy and California's Governor Jerry Brown portrayed Carter as weak in a time of national crisis. Seeking to reassure the public that he was a bold leader, Carter used the American grain trade to the Soviet Union to make his stand.

Secretary of Agriculture Bob Bergland warned that in the event of a grain embargo against the Soviet Union, American farmers would be the losers. Bergland estimated $3.5 billion in lost revenues as well as damaged trading relationships with other nations who would see that the United States could not be relied upon to fulfill contracts. Carter, however, promised to use $2.6 billion to purchase the embargoed wheat and corn through the Commodity Credit Corporation, thereby covering any lost income. To ease the fears of wheat and corn farmers, Carter declared, "I am determined to minimize any adverse impact on the American farmer from this action. The undeliverable grain will be removed from the market through storage and price support programs and through purchases at market prices." He also promised, "We will also increase amounts of grain devoted to the alleviation of hunger in poor countries, and we'll have a massive increase in the use of grain for gasohol production here at home."

On January 3 the Soviets, anticipating Carter's decision, purchased 2.7 million tons of corn and 400,000 tons of wheat. When the president announced the grain embargo the next day, he disallowed that purchase and agreed to honor only the 8 million tons of grain that the Soviets had purchased earlier under the five-year bilateral Grain and Oil Trade Agreement signed in October 1975. Consequently Carter's embargo applied to 17 million tons of grain. Its success depended on the cooperation of other grain-exporting nations, particularly Canada, Australia, and Argentina. Canada and Australia agreed not to ship more grain to the Soviets than "normal and traditional" quantities, while Argentina, then harvesting a large wheat crop, lacking storage facilities, and needing foreign currency, refused to honor the embargo.

After Carter announced the grain embargo, the prices of corn, wheat, and soybeans (which were also included in the ban) fell significantly before rebounding to pre-embargo levels two weeks later, largely because of federal price-support purchases through the Commodity Credit Corporation. Even so, grain farmers and the politicians who represented them were distinctly unhappy. Senator Robert Dole of Kansas, then campaigning for the presidency, called the embargo a "devastating impact on American farmers and on taxpayers generally." On a more visceral level, Dole charged that "Mr. Carter took a poke at the Russian bear and kicked the American farmer in the teeth." Republican presidential hopeful George Bush said, "Farmers have been asked to do more than other Americans." Senator Ted Kennedy of Massachusetts agreed, saying on the campaign trail, "A grain embargo won't work. The Soviet troops won't leave Afghanistan, and the American farmer will pay the price for an ineffective foreign policy."

At first many farmers supported the embargo, but they soon agreed with the political opposition. Russell Arndt, president of the National Corn Growers Association, charged that the "cutoff of sales and delivery of grain to the USSR is the heaviest blow to American agricultural producers, agribusiness, and the agricultural community since the Great Depression." Earl Hunt, president of the Kansas Wheat Growers Association agreed, contending that "The Kansas farmer would sure want to be 100 percent behind the President at this critical time, but most of the farmers that I've talked to . . . are just stunned." Another wheat grower reflected that "we shouldn't have to go broke being patriotic," while one farmer complained that "we would like to see everyone sacrifice too." Farmers' magazines predicted nothing but long-term negative consequences from the grain embargo.

Perceptions, of course, are more important than reality. Argentina, Australia, Canada, and other nations covered the 17 million tons of embargoed grain from the United States. But when those countries sold that tonnage of grain to the Soviet Union, they could not meet other market demands, and the United States sold much of the grain initially reserved for the Soviets to other nations that would have purchased from the countries now trading with the Russians. As a result, total U.S. grain exports *rose* during the embargo. In other words, while grain farmers complained, federal policy in effect simply redirected grain flows while maintaining price levels to the farmers' advantage.

No matter. By the presidential election of 1980 the grain

embargo epitomized for many the problems of American agriculture, particularly the ineptitude and failure of federal farm policy. Although the government compensated grain farmers for the loss of the Soviet market, they chose to believe otherwise. Farmers had come to expect the federal government to aid them overtly, not to adopt a policy that suggested sacrifice on their part. As a result, on election day in 1980 many farmers turned to Ronald Reagan to save them, and on April 24, 1981, he ended the embargo.

AGRICULTURAL ORGANIZATIONS

During the late twentieth century the major agricultural organizations continued to advocate their traditional plans to increase farm income. The Farm Bureau, for example, favored lower price supports and loans to small-scale farmers through existing credit programs to help them gain other employment and leave the farm. It also urged the federal government to increase the sale of agricultural commodities through Public Law 480, grant loans to developing nations through the Commodity Credit Corporation, and seek the expansion of foreign markets. The Farm Bureau supported acreage reduction and promoted the use of grain for the production of industrial alcohol and gasohol (also known as ethanol) to reduce the supply of grain. It urged credit institutions to proceed slowly with foreclosures. It also supported the revision of tax laws to prohibit investments in agriculture for tax purposes alone.

In contrast the Farmers' Union continued to favor a commodity-by-commodity approach to prices and production controls, 100 percent parity for milk, reduction in federal controls, expansion of international marketing agreements to improve foreign sales, legislation to protect small-scale farmers from low prices, and laws to prevent nonfarm corporations from engaging in agriculture. The Farmers' Union also supported legislation designed to provide farmers with the bargaining power that would make them a "countervailing force" to the economic power of corporate America. For its part, the Grange favored limiting government payments to $20,000 annually for any farmer or corporation, the prohibition of tax shelters in agriculture for nonfarmers or nonfarm corporations, expansion of foreign trade, parity income, a producer-managed marketing program, acreage reductions, and federal crop loans.

While the differences among these farm organizations chiefly concerned the degree of federal involvement in agriculture, two agricultural organizations—the National Farmers' Organization and the American Agriculture Movement—dramatized the militancy felt by some farmers. Since its organization in 1955, the NFO had advocated a union of farmers to give them bargaining power in the marketplace. It had aimed to negotiate with food processors and other buyers of agricultural commodities for contracts that ensured cost-of-production returns plus a small profit. The NFO believed that through the power of collective action—by withholding their commodities from market, much like the activities of the Farmers' Holiday Association—they could force buyers to meet their demands. The NFO estimated that it needed to organize 25 percent of the farmers in a given area, who controlled at least 60 percent of a commodity, for successful action.

After buyers persistently refused to negotiate contracts with the NFO to guarantee cost-of-production prices plus a profit, in early September 1962 the organization began a "withholding action." It began by holding livestock off the market to force meatpackers to bargain with the organization. Many NFO members lined the roads and used violence to prevent the shipment of livestock to market by other farmers. By early October, however, the strike had collapsed because members could not afford to keep their cattle and hogs from market. In 1967 the NFO sponsored a milk strike and won considerable national attention with images in the news magazines of farmers dumping milk in roadside ditches. A year later the NFO sponsored a cattle kill in which several hundred cattle, including calves, were shot before cameras to emphasize that farmers could not afford to raise livestock at below cost-of-production prices. This violence gained more negative than positive publicity for the NFO, and it made many farmers reluctant to join the organization. It dramatized, however, the economic plight of many farmers, particularly in the Midwest. Since the 1970s the NFO has emphasized its marketing program; sought 90 percent of parity on commodity loans; favored the release of government reserves only in time of national emergency; and advocated a world floor price agreement among the grain-exporting nations, federal legislation permitting farmers to form strong bargaining and marketing associations, and the prohibition of nonfarm corporations from engaging in agriculture.

The radical activities of the National Farmers' Organization gave way to the American Agriculture Movement (AAM) a decade later. In 1977 the AAM emerged from the wheat region of the Great Plains and quickly spread across the Midwest and South. Once again farmers began to hear calls for a farm strike, during which time they would neither buy nor sell. The AAM took a militant tone by demanding 100 percent of parity for all agricultural products produced and consumed in the United States. Unless all agricultural organizations agreed to support this goal, the AAM threatened to cancel all memberships and insurance held in those organizations, such as the Farm Bureau. The AAM presented this "ultimatum" to Congress with a December 14 deadline for action. If Congress failed to approve legislation mandating 100 percent parity agricultural prices, the AAM pledged to strike by not planting crops in 1978. Defiantly the members proclaimed, "We the farmers of this nation will halt all agricultural production and distribution immediately. This action will continue until our demands are met."

Using protest techniques learned from their sons and daughters in the 1960s, AAM members began to demonstrate for higher prices while displaying signs that read "Parity Not Charity" and "Crime Doesn't Pay. Neither Does Farming." A new word—tractorcade—appeared in the language. Television audiences watched as farmers paraded their heavy equipment through the nation's capital to gain support for increased parity prices. Although most farmers did not identify with the AAM's goal of 100 percent parity price supports, they were sympathetic—and dissatisfied with the level of farm prices and government aid. While unwilling to support a farm strike, many farmers held their own tractorcades during the late 1970s. Some farmers talked about cutting production by reducing spring planting by half unless they received 100 percent parity prices. Most farmers, however, could not or would not take that risk without a guarantee of price increases. No single farmer could make an impact by acting alone, and farmers were too independent, too conservative, and too diverse in their needs to act collectively.

Although the major farm organizations could not reach agreement on a solution for the farm problem in the late twentieth century, farmers felt abandoned when government policymakers heard the pleas of other strong pressure groups, such as environmentalists or consumers. Many farmers across regions and commodities felt the loss of political power that comes with minority status. They looked to the federal government to improve agricultural conditions by expanding foreign markets and reducing its involvement in agriculture. These contradictory desires were typical of farmers nationwide. They wanted government aid if it was advantageous but opposed it if that aid threatened to diminish their independence or potential profits. Most farmers believed that their economic conditions could be improved if most of the middlemen were eliminated from the marketing process, thereby enabling farmers to market more directly while keeping food prices low for consumers. They also believed that consumers and small-scale businesspeople potentially were their best allies, while environmentalists, big business, organized labor, and the urban poor represented threats to the agricultural community.

SCIENCE AND TECHNOLOGY

Scientific and technological change continued to drive agricultural production during the late twentieth century. Often this technology involved systems rather than individual pieces of hardware such as tractors or chemicals. The adoption of the cotton picker, for example, required agricultural scientists to develop a cotton plant that ripened uniformly and grew to a standard height so that the machine could pick the lint easily in a once-over operation. The tomato harvester also did not become practical until scientists developed a tomato that could withstand the machine's rough handling, and even those tomatoes were suitable only for sauces and paste rather than for slicing at the table. Much of the technological change during the late twentieth century was evolutionary rather than revolutionary: it built on the achievements of the past.

Tractors did not change fundamentally, but they became bigger to enable farmers to cover more land, often acquired after their neighbors went out of business. Tractors became the key to mechanization on the farm, because these implements had a multiplier effect. With large tractors, farmers could plow, plant, and harvest more acres with other implements specifically designed for certain jobs. Expanded acreage, in turn, often meant the consolidation of farms and fewer farmers. Tractors also enhanced specialization. Tractors and accompanying implements, however, required a large capital investment, and farmers usually purchased this equipment with loans from local banks. They attempted to pay for these implements by reducing costs and increasing production, usually by specializing in one or two crops, such as wheat, corn, cotton, or soybeans, which produced the greatest volume and reduced unit costs.

Dairy farmers improved their herds with artificial insemination. New methods for collecting, storing, and freezing semen contributed to this technological advance. Artificial insemination helped maintain genetic diversity in dairy herds. Dairy farmers also began using improved feed that had been scientifically developed for superior nutrition. In 1990 dairy farmers adopted the recombinant DNA bovine somatotropin (bST), a synthetic hormone which boosted milk production by as much as 25 percent in well-managed herds. Dairy cows no longer roamed the pastures but remained in drylots, where they ate before moving to the barns for milking by machines three times a day. During the 1960s scientists also developed semi-dwarf wheat varieties that did not clog the combine nor shatter from the heads before the grain reached the threshing cylinder. Overall farmers relied more and more on machines to reduce their labor costs, and they used chemicals to increase production and reduce losses to pests and disease.

Despite these technological improvements, farmers continued to rely on government to solve their scientific and technological problems. Federal- and state-supported researchers at the University of California at Davis, for example, developed the tomato harvester. In 1972 Congress created the Office of Technology Assessment to investigate the economic, social, and environmental consequences of new technologies such as bST. A year later the Food and Drug Administration banned the use of the growth hormone diethylstilbestrol (DES) as a feed additive for beef cattle because research indicated that it caused cancer.

Until the 1970s farmers tended to support the development of manufactured solutions, such as chemicals and new plant varieties and animal breeds, for their specific problems. After that time they generally favored a combination of biotechnology and computer and systems-management technologies, such as conservation tillage and grazing management, to produce as efficiently and as productively as possible. At the same time the consolidation of seed companies threatened to increase operating costs for farmers as fewer companies offered their products on the market. Some farmers feared that the seed and chemical companies would develop plants that were resistant only to the company's herbicides, not the weed killers of competitors. Many critics also charged that biotechnology threatened to create new, undreamed-of problems for both farmers and city dwellers.

American agriculture changed rapidly after World War II. Technology and science enabled farmers to become more productive than ever before. As productivity increased, only the most efficient farmers were able to marshal the resources needed to maintain their operation in an economy in which they had no control over the prices they received. As a result, despite rhetoric about the value of farm life, thousands of young men and women fled the farm for the city. Their parents frequently encouraged them to go—and many parents left too. Government programs helped large-scale farmers stay on the land, but small-scale farmers often were unable to obtain the financial support they needed. Farmers remained dependent on the federal government for income through price supports, marketing help, and acreage-reduction programs. Yet these programs worked to the advantage of large-scale farmers, enabling them to purchase more land and equipment and thereby farm more extensively and efficiently while forcing small-scale, noncompetitive, or unprofitable farmers from the land. Given these problems, one should not be surprised at the number of people who left the farms. Rather, one should be amazed at the number who remained.

The largest producers received the greatest income support from federal farm programs. The Food Security Act of 1985, for example, enabled J. G. Boswell, a California company and one of the largest producers of cotton, to collect nearly $20 million in subsidies annually. A spokesman for Boswell defended these government payments, saying, "It is ludicrous to believe that we will be sticking any Government money in our pockets. This is survival money." Robert Thompson, assistant secretary of agriculture for economics, offered a different opinion, suggesting that these farm corporations "may get looked upon as the welfare queens." Between 1985 and 1987 government spending for price and income supports increased from $17.8 billion to an estimated $35 billion, largely due to price-supporting subsidy payments, such as loans through the Commodity Credit Corporation, which essentially put a floor under commodity prices.

In 1985 the large-scale farms that sold more than $500,000 worth of products annually received approximately 15 percent of all federal payments, though those farms comprised only 2 percent of the total. Still, 85 percent of the payments went to smaller-scale farm operations, and about 60 percent of the payments went to farmers with financial problems, such as high debt and poor cash flow. Put differently, most farmers who participated in government programs received between $22,000 and $24,000 annually. Nevertheless the large corporate farms that produced cotton and rice, not the smaller-scale operators who raised corn and wheat, received the most money from the federal government.

Under the Food Security Act the federal government also paid dairy farmers to slaughter or export their herds in order to reduce production. The De Graaf Family Dairy in California received an estimated $10 million to get out of the business. In California, farmers in the Central Valley used irrigation water heavily subsidized by the federal government to raise crops that were also subsidized—the process was called "double dipping." One wheat and soybean farmer in Iowa remarked, "To put it very bluntly, if you're not farming the Government today, you're not doing a very good job."

By the late 1980s nearly 42 percent of the farmland in the United States was operated under rental agreements. This was the greatest extent of farmland rented since the Dust Bowl years of the 1930s, when tenants operated nearly 45 percent of the farmland nationwide. Given high operating costs and low returns, as well as escalating land prices which made it difficult for young people to begin farming, many agriculturists preferred to rent their land to other farmers who often operated on a large scale. By 1990 only 4.5 million farmers remained on the land, down from 32.1 million in 1935. Their average age remained about 50, as it had since the 1950s. But only the large-scale farmers were profitable; medium-sized farms, those that most people considered family-sized, were barely able to break even. Small-scale farms, which were the most numerous, usually lost money, sometimes suffered bankruptcy, and often ended up being rented to large-scale operators.

By the mid-1990s, when American agricultural policy underwent significant, even seismic, change, about 2 million farmers comprised only 1.7 percent of the total population. They operated 2,196,000 farms that averaged about 438 acres. Gross farm income reached $210 billion while gross net income totaled about $37 billion, with total government payments reaching more than $7 billion. In 1995 net income per farm averaged only $11,218 from agricultural business while government subsidies contributed about $24,000 per farm. Farmers also averaged another $39,671 from off-farm employment. The off-farm employment gave farmers 98.8 percent of the average household income in the United States. On a scale of 100, farmers received an index price of 102 for all commodities sold, but they paid an index price of 109 for all farming costs. At the same time nearly all the New Deal agricultural legislation remained in effect, based on the Agricultural Adjustment Act of 1938 as amended by the Agricultural Act of 1949. These policies continued to create surpluses, force people from the land, reduce the number of farms, increase mechanization, and contribute to the decline of small-scale family farms while encouraging, even demanding, the dependency of farmers on the federal government for survival and expanding the regulatory state in American agriculture.

Critics have argued that federal farm programs prompted farmers to produce those commodities for which they could receive guaranteed income from the federal government through a number of programs. These income-support programs encouraged maximum production which in turn fostered environmentally damaging practices that led to soil erosion and water pollution, among other environmental problems. Critics also charged that farm programs placed a heavy burden on taxpayers and kept inefficient farmers on the land. Farm consolidation, fewer farmers, and fewer subsidies, they argued, offered the best hope of ensuring an adequate food supply while enabling the remaining farmers to earn a profit. Critics also contended that subsidies, in the form of deficiency payments when target prices were not met, encouraged farmers to bid up land prices as they attempted to acquire more acreage and, with more fertilizer and machinery, increase production in order to collect more subsidies on a greater volume of production. When larger expenditures for land, fertilizer, and equipment ate up subsidy income, farmers asked the government to do more for them. The farm organizations also were unwilling to give up subsidies as long as other nations subsidized their farmers and permitted them to sell relatively cheaply on the world market yet still receive an adequate income. At the very least, farmers wanted the federal government to stabilize farm income if not enhance farm profits, no matter whether it used high or flexible price supports, acreage reductions, or subsidized world marketing.

By 1996, however, Republicans in control of both houses of Congress were dedicated to weaning farmers from government programs and committing agriculture to a market-oriented economy. The percentage of net farm income derived from government payments and the percentage of cropland withdrawn from production by government programs had not declined since the 1960s. By the mid-1990s, 21 percent of net farm income came from government payments for participation in a variety of price-support, acreage-reduction, and other programs, while 23 percent of available cropland was idled under government programs.

In 1996 the highest crop prices in twenty years led Congress to revise agricultural policy radically. Republicans argued that price supports and acreage-reduction programs dating from the New Deal had encouraged surplus production, farm consolidations, flight from the land, and rural poverty while placing an enormous burden on taxpayers and the Treasury. The new legislation, the Federal Agriculture Improvement and Reform Act (FAIR) or, colloquially, the Freedom to Farm Act, was the first major change in farm policy since 1949. It provided for a systematic reduction in federal payments to farmers over seven years, regardless of the amount of commodity surpluses or the level of market prices. At the end of seven years farmers would no longer receive payments in any form for production. Meanwhile they could produce any crop in any amount, though previous contracts for withdrawing acreage from production under the Conservation Reserve Program remained in force. Republican Senator Richard Luger, chairman of the Senate Committee on Agriculture, Forestry, and Nutrition, declared that the FAIR Act would "change agricultural policy more fundamentally than any law in sixty years."

With commodity prices high, most farmers welcomed this legislation. It provided seven years of price supports and gave them the right to unlimited production. Few realized, however, that at the end of seven years, if not before, the federal "safety net" would be gone, after which they could no longer depend on the government for income support. For the moment, however, they had the best of both worlds—unlimited production and price supports. Those farmers who saw potential danger no doubt believed they could still demand support from the federal government if hard times returned. History gave them every reason to continue their reliance on the federal government.

6

Century's End

AT THE END of the twentieth century, the world of the American farmer had been transformed since 1900. In the South, few farmers, black or white, remained. Technology, government policy, and economic change had pushed or pulled most Southerners from the land. Those who remained often needed off-farm employment to maintain an adequate standard of living as well as subsidize their farming operations. Southern agriculture was far different at the turn of the twenty-first century than when the twentieth century began. In 1900 poor whites and blacks with little capital, land, and technology typified the farmers in the region, and sharecropping and tenancy prevailed. By 2000 sharecropping had been gone for a long time. In many areas where cotton and tobacco once grew in abundance, soybeans provided the major cash crop while lush pastures supported grazing beef cattle. Cotton was no longer king.

Northeastern farmers specialized in dairying and potatoes. Some farmers had diversified by growing cranberries and blueberries as well as sweet corn and apples, which they sold directly to consumers at roadside stands and farmers' markets. Others raised flowers and shrubs, which they marketed from their nurseries and greenhouses. Some farmers had resurrected cooperative marketing for the sale of vegetables to supermarket chains. Suburban sprawl, however, steadily absorbed farmland while the countryside became increasingly populated with people fleeing urban life, but who had no intention of becoming farmers.

In the Midwest, grain, soybeans, and livestock predominated. There wheat and corn farmers received a disproportionate percentage of agricultural subsidies, and they remained vocal and politically powerful through their organizations. Yet government subsidies kept land prices high because many farmers used this income to purchase or rent more land in order to raise more crops and receive more subsidies. Hog and poultry farmers increasingly became contract producers for the major processors. This vertical integration reduced their capital investments but deprived them of freedom of action because they followed the production orders of the buyers who provided a guaranteed market. Large-scale hog facilities invariably brought complaints of odor nuisances and polluted streams and rivers. Nonfarm residents also worried that heavy applications of nitrogen fertilizer contaminated underground water supplies.

In the Far West, California led the nation in cotton production. West Coast and Arizona farmers also raised abundant crops of rice, fruits, and vegetables. Urban expansion, however, increased property taxes and forced many farmers to sell their lands to developers; city demands for water became an ongoing battle with growers. Large-scale fruit and vegetable farms defined specialty production while vertical integration typified the big business, capital-intensive nature of farming in California.

THE NEW CENTURY

By the turn of the twenty-first century, farmers comprised only 1.6 percent of the population, or 4.4 million people.

In 1999, after more than six decades of consolidations, the number of farms had dwindled to 2,190,070, with an average of 432 acres. Gross farm income reached $235.5 billion while gross net income totaled more than $43.3 billion. Government payments for participation in various programs contributed $20.5 billion to farm income. Net income per farm averaged $13,194, but off-farm income contributed another $57,988 to the farm operation, which usually meant that both husband and wife worked off the farm. A year later the number of farms declined to 2,172,080, with an average of 434 acres. In 2002, if the index of 1990–1992 = 100 is used, the parity rate for prices received by farmers reached 97 while they paid an index price of 119—a parity ratio of 81 percent. If the 1909–1914 index is used, the parity ratio between prices paid and received dropped to 39 percent.

If farms with $100,000 or more in annual sales are considered "commercial" farms, only 16.7 percent of the total number of farms can be so classified, but these "commercial" farms produced approximately 80 percent of all agricultural commodities. At the same time approximately 62 percent of direct cash payments from the federal government went to farmers with annual gross sales of $100,000 or more, because payments were based on volume. The largest-scale farmers, in other words, had the greatest opportunity to profit from government programs for reducing production, through target prices, deficiency payments, and price-supporting loans from the Commodity Credit Corporation. Off-farm income averaged nearly 65 percent of total farm income. As the farm population continued to decline, the *Wall Street Journal* observed that federal farm programs had failed to save the "beloved species" of the American farmer.

Although the FAIR Act of 1996 attempted to transform agricultural policy by making it more market oriented while removing target prices, deficiency payments, and acreage-reduction programs, and helping Republicans balance the federal budget, the act met with considerable opposition. Some critics called the Federal Agriculture Improvement and Reform (FAIR) Act "fairy tale" legislation that amounted to nothing more than "welfare payments" to the large-scale farmers who were represented in Congress by the major agricultural organizations, commodity groups, and agribusiness industry.

The FAIR Act encouraged farmers to capitalize on high market prices by planting as many acres as possible through 2002 while simultaneously receiving government program checks. This increased production glutted international markets, and along with faltering Asian and Latin American economies, depressed agricultural prices to thirty-year lows. Declining price supports further reduced farm income. Congress apparently overlooked or forgot that the FAIR Act had not repealed the Agricultural Adjustment Act of 1938 as amended by the Agricultural Act of 1949. Consequently that New Deal–inspired legislation remained available for Congress to implement if the FAIR Act failed to meet farmers' needs.

In 1998 Congress responded accordingly by providing emergency payments to farmers, thereby doubling instead of reducing the cost of the farm program and making government payments about half of net farm income. Yet 150,000 of the largest farmers received nearly half that money. Approximately 80 percent of farm payments went to large- and medium-scale farmers.

FARM SUBSIDIES

After considerable complaining and lobbying about the inadequacies of the FAIR Act, Congress provided a record $32.3 billion in agricultural subsidies to farmers by the autumn of 2000. As a result, even though Congress had promised to reduce government payments in the 1996 farm legislation, farmers became even more dependent on the federal government. Secretary of Agriculture Dan Glickman told a conference of Women Involved in Farm Economics, "We're going to spend the highest amount of dollars ever in the history of American agriculture." In 1998 the emergency aid provided to farmers ended any pretense that agriculture would be cast into a free-market economy. Secretary Glickman said of the emergency aid, "I'm not telling you it's going to be heaven on earth, but there's an awful lot of money flowing out there." Congress proved generous once again. The federal government estimated that previous programs, such as conservation payments and price-supporting loans that generated farm income, together with the new, emergency subsidies, would provide farmers with about 40 percent of their income for 2000, a 2 percent increase from the preceding year. Wheat, corn, cotton, and rice farmers received most of these program subsidies to help them recover from low commodity prices.

This late-twentieth-century bailout can be largely attributed to the collapse of agricultural exports in the wake of large harvests worldwide and economic recessions in Asia and Latin America, and the sharp decline of domestic prices due to overproduction at home. Some aid, however, involved disaster relief in response to drought, hurricanes, and floods. By 2001 the USDA had issued $71 billion in "emergency bailout" cash payments to farmers, totaling more than three times the amount they were scheduled to receive under the FAIR Act. Congress also raised the limit on government subsidies and emergency aid from $40,000 per person to $460,000 per farm annually. Farmers could receive even more federal support if they could add their children as owners when contracting for various farm programs. The USDA made these emergency payments to farmers based on the average production of their past crops.

By century's end some farmers had left agriculture and no longer planted crops. Yet they could still apply for federal agricultural subsidies because they remained landowners. President Bill Clinton opposed this relief aid distribution program and proposed that Congress authorize the USDA to pay farmers only if they planted crops, targeting those farmers who most needed economic help. But Congress, seeing the political liability of appearing unresponsive to the severe economic crisis on the farms, did not act on the president's request.

GENETICALLY MODIFIED CROPS

By the late twentieth century, plant breeders had proven that they could genetically alter plants to fortify them with added vitamins and minerals, and to resist weeds, pests, and disease. They could also alter plants to mature at certain times, tolerate specific climates, and improve harvesting, among other changes. As a result, consumers with dietary deficiencies could benefit from genetically engineered crops while farmers reduced their costs through specialized and more dependable production.

By 2000, however, some farmers questioned whether they *should* grow genetically modified organisms (GMOs). Several food-processing companies refused to purchase these crops, and farmers had to keep the harvested commodities isolated from nongenetically modified crops for purposes of sale. Some opponents of genetically modified crops argued that the biotechnology industry had misled farmers and the public into believing that GMOs would solve the problem of world hunger while improving agricultural efficiency and increasing profits. Soybeans, for example, engineered to resist certain herbicides, limited a farmer to the use of only one herbicide, usually produced or sold by the company that developed the seeds for the resulting crop. Farmers were now caught in a dilemma. They wanted to increase production and lower herbicide costs and dependency, but if they had to purchase seeds and herbicides from the same source, their costs could substantially increase because they were a captive market.

By the end of the century this debate over the profitability, safety, and efficiency of genetically modified crops had not ended. Farmers and seed and chemical companies sparred with consumers over the safety of genetically modified crops in the production of foods for consumers. The debate over the safety of genetically modified crops also indicated the increased dependence of the American farmer on international markets. Although genetically modified crops, such as corn and soybeans, enabled farmers to improve their chances for a profitable harvest by planting crops that would resist drought and common pests, European consumers particularly rejected American-produced genetically modified or biotech (Bt) corn. Asian consumers also began to question the safety of these crops in the food chain, while environmentalists, organic producers, and opponents of Bt crops worried that continued use would cause pests to develop an immunity or resistance that might spread to other high-tech crops. Even Food and Drug Administration (FDA)–approved Bt crops, such as the Flavr-Savr tomato, which permitted longer vine ripening, redder color, and more flavor, faced consumer opposition because it was a "genetically engineered" rather than a "natural" crop.

By the spring of 2000 major food processors such as Frito-Lay, Gerber Products Co., and Archer Daniels Midland had stopped buying genetically engineered ingredients, or demanded that they be kept separate from nonbiotech products. As a result, Starlink corn, developed by Aventis CropScience, became a major issue. Starlink contained a protein fatal to European corn borers, and in 1998 the FDA approved it for livestock feed. But the FDA did not authorize it for human consumption because some research indicated that Starlink could cause allergic reactions. A report from the Centers for Disease Control and Prevention, however, found no evidence that eating food with Bt corn would make people sick.

At the same time some researchers showed that Bt corn killed monarch butterflies when they ate its pollen. Other scientists argued that Bt corn posed little risk to monarchs because the pollen was not toxic in concentrations that the larvae of these butterflies encountered in nature. These charges and countercharges about the safety of Bt crops further alarmed consumers and environmentalists.

After grain buyers, accidentally or otherwise, sold some Starlink corn to food processors, Kraft Foods recalled its taco shells made from corn contaminated by Starlink flour. Farmers who raised Starlink corn lost sales, and many demanded compensation from Aventis because domestic and foreign buyers had refused to accept their product. Ultimately, in early 2000, the USDA agreed to spend $20 million to remove all Bt or Starlink seed corn from the market, and Aventis made a multi-million-dollar settlement with farmers and elevator operators who had bought its product but had lost markets and money for raising or accepting it. A group of food companies also agreed to attach $6 million in coupons, each worth $1, to food products that had contained Starlink corn in order to win back customers. By the late twentieth century, Bt wheat was still several years away from development, but European buyers had already told American shippers they would not buy it.

In early 2000 Burger King also announced that it would not buy french fries processed from genetically altered potatoes, and Gerber Products Company opposed its biotech parent, Novartis, and declined to purchase biotech crops for its baby foods. Some consumer advocates demanded the labeling of GMO foods while others sought the irradiation of all foods to ensure their safety and protect consumer health.

Small-scale farmers worried whether they could remain in

business if the seed companies sold only expensive, genetically altered seed because they could not produce sufficiently large crops to avoid a cost-price squeeze. Some critics argued that if only large- or medium-scale farmers could afford biotechnology, the small-scale "family farmer" would essentially disappear. The agribusiness corporations would control the food supply with resulting higher prices. While the biotech companies countered that their seeds would improve production and profits for all farmers, small-scale farmers believed that biotech products put them on the "bleeding edge" rather than the "cutting edge" of agricultural science.

Although high fuel costs encouraged farmers to plant genetically modified crops that would allow them to cultivate their fields less frequently, consumers were more concerned about food safety. By century's end the major food-processing companies had begun to listen to consumers and prepare their foods accordingly. A spokesman for the USDA explained, "The customer is king or queen. Eventually customers around the world are going to be the ones who decide the extent to which they are going to embrace or ignore biotech crops." Farmers were still subject to forces beyond their control.

Early in 2002, for example, the Sierra Club joined with Friends of the Earth and several consumer-action groups to pressure Kraft Foods to stop marketing foods in the United States produced from genetically engineered crops. Kraft had met European consumer demands by marketing foods free from genetically engineered ingredients on the continent. The Sierra Club also asked Kraft to stop using milk from cows treated with genetically engineered bovine growth hormones. Although Kraft contended that all its food products were safe, any policy change by this company was closely watched by many soybean and dairy farmers: three-fourths of the soybean crop had been genetically modified, and most milk came from cows that had been treated with hormones to enhance production. One Sierra Club official contended that genetically engineered ingredients in human food made "guinea pigs" of the American public. Little wonder that farmers worried about the relationships of science and technology to markets and production decisions.

AGRIBUSINESS

A number of corporate mergers near the close of the century affected farmers. New Holland, a Dutch-based manufacturer of farm equipment, purchased the Case Corporation, thereby creating a new, formidable competitor for the industry leader, John Deere & Company, but also limiting farmers' competitive choices. By the end of the century at least eighteen of the world's largest petrochemical and pharmaceutical companies had acquired interests in seed companies, including Imperial Chemical Industries of Britain, which purchased the Garst Seed Company, and Ciba-Geigy, a major U.S. chemical producer, which bought Funk Seeds International. DuPont acquired Pioneer Hi-Bred International, the largest seed corn company in the world. Some farmers believed this merger would reduce their choices, because Monsanto had already acquired DeKalb Genetic Corporation, Holden's Foundation Seeds, Hyritech Seed International, and Asgrow Seed Company. Cargill, the global grain, oilseed, and meat processor and trader, acquired the grain storage, transportation, export, and trading operations of its rival, Continental Grain Company. Bayer Ag of Germany bought Aventis CropScience. The days of the small-scale, locally or family owned seed, equipment, and meat-processing companies lay in the distant past. International or multinational corporations now touched the daily lives of American farm men and women and largely determined what farmers bought and sold.

Agribusiness mergers increased the economic and scientific

power of the corporations involved, especially in the development of genetically altered products. Some scientists and environmentalists warned that the petrochemical/seed companies, through their research and marketing, would force farmers who bought their seed also to purchase their herbicides—all of it leading to greater chemical use and more environmental pollution. Others argued that such mergers would enhance scientific and technological research to such a degree that farmers would gain still greater productivity. Yet while improved productivity might reduce food prices, continued surplus production would further reduce commodity prices.

THE ENVIRONMENT, SOCIETY, AND PUBLIC HEALTH

By the end of the twentieth century the nonfarming public, including those who lived in urban as well as rural areas, had become increasingly concerned about agricultural practices that endangered or might threaten public health. These concerns superseded economics. They included, for example, the safety of drinking water and the preservation of wetlands and wildlife habitat. Environmental policy had become an important and highly visible public issue for rural areas, and it no longer remained the provenance of farmers.

Urban voters in many respects controlled the environmental agenda; farmers, who numbered considerably fewer than town and city dwellers, confronted policy issues over which they had diminished control. The public no longer considered agriculture "special"; at best it was suspect, with farmers often regarded as the major environmental polluters in the countryside. Urban interests wanted a greater voice in regulating farming practices, particularly the livestock industry. Residents of Des Moines, Iowa; Raleigh, North Carolina; and North Platte, Nebraska, for example, did not wish to relax in their backyards on a summer evening and smell a cattle feedlot or a hog confinement facility, or the peculiar aroma that comes from the fertilization of land with manure. They were not concerned about volume, unit cost, and efficiency, only about unpleasant odors. Moreover, cattle feedlots and hog confinement facilities often depressed property values in nearby towns, and they sometimes contaminated rivers and streams from runoff. The nonfarming public demanded clean water for daily life, and that meant governmental regulation of farmers to prevent contamination of drinking water from fertilizers, pesticides, and herbicides. Investors in recreational and tourist areas also wanted livestock confinement facilities kept beyond "smelling distance." Some scientists even advocated state regulation of odors and noxious chemicals emitted from livestock facilities.

Sharp divisions developed between farmers and their organizations, and consumers and scientists. Some producers argued that odors were merely annoying, even a nuisance, but smell did not create a health risk. Their opponents pointed to evidence that hydrogen sulfide and ammonia emissions from livestock confinements caused respiratory problems for workers in those facilities, while phosphorus from poultry manure caused algae problems in nearby streams. County governments increasingly fought with state legislatures over regulatory control of factory farms and corporate livestock and poultry confinement operations while environmental groups demanded strict regulation of such facilities. In some areas residents mobilized to block the establishment of poultry and livestock operations, particularly near tourist areas, despite the potential boost to the local economy by the creation of jobs. At the end of the century, many of these disputes still required judicial resolution. Most experts agreed that manure lagoons leaked, but they could not agree on how much seepage into rivers, streams, and underground water supplies was unhealthy.

Farmers came to realize that consumers would increasingly shape agricultural policy in the new century. Consumers wanted food that saved time and promoted health (instead of just providing nutrition) by protecting them against heart disease and cancer. Domestic and foreign consumers also demanded foods that promoted social objectives such as environmental quality.

Although scientific research had not proven that beef and dairy cattle treated with growth hormones (with the exception of DES) or genetically modified corn and soybeans were hazardous to human health, many consumers, domestic and foreign, did not care to eat hormone-treated beef or genetically altered corn or soybeans. Consumers' rejections of these agricultural products may have been based on poor science, but their perceptions were decisive. Farmers began halting the production of those commodities because they could not market them easily, if at all.

A New Agricultural Policy

Although the FAIR Act of 1996 attempted to end agricultural subsidies based on acreage reductions and price supports, it failed to protect farm income from surplus production and falling prices. Loopholes in the act enabled the largest-scale farmers to reap most of the remaining subsidies. At the same time a collapsing agricultural economy necessitated congressional action that provided millions of dollars in emergency aid to farmers, thereby making a mockery of the FAIR Act.

As the farm economy collapsed, Congress continued to listen to those farm, commodity, and agribusiness organizations that still comprised an influential Farm Bloc. Democrats advocated a return to high support prices while Republicans favored giving farmers more emergency money. Both parties wanted a "safety net" for farmers. By 1999 the USDA provided approximately $6 billion in direct payments to farmers, including deficiency payments, and about $5 billion in loans from the Commodity Credit Corporation. Congress also provided $6 billion in emergency aid to help farmers suffering from low prices and weather-related crop losses. Farmers also received $2 billion for putting some 30.5 million acres into the Conservation Reserve Program. Inequity prevailed in this distribution of federal largess: livestock, fruit, and vegetable producers, who earned nearly 60 percent of the agricultural cash revenue, received no direct federal aid.

Some agricultural experts urged Congress to craft a new farm policy that favored people more than commodities. They called for Congress to pay farmers a minimum wage that would equal what they could make in full-time employment, thereby shifting the emphasis from commodities to labor— that is, from grains to people. Dissatisfaction prevailed because $27 billion in emergency subsidies were doled out in 2000 to just 10 percent of farm owners, including multi-million-dollar corporations, government agencies, and individuals. Those funds went to aid wealthy landowners such as billionaire Ted Turner, professional athletes, and an heir to the Rockefeller fortune. Some of the wealthiest members of Congress also profited from the emergency farm legislation they themselves approved, as well as twenty Fortune 500 companies, university and prison farms, and real estate developers.

Small-scale farmers argued that government payments did not save family farmers. They received too little while the large-scale operators received too much. In California, for example, most of the state's $480 million in rice subsidies went to large farms operated by extended families. In 2000 nineteen of those farms received $1 million in federal subsidies, while ninety-three received between $500,000 and $1 million. One rice grower reflected, "The market doesn't pay us enough to stay in business," but the government "dole" kept them in agriculture.

Nationally, about 60 percent of farm subsidies went to 10 percent of all farmers, particularly grain and cotton producers. As federal aid increasingly supported farmers with powerful commodity organizations and political supporters, many small-scale farmers received barely enough to remain viable. Many farmers who looked to the government for aid and expected it were disappointed and left the land. Of those farmers who remained, approximately two-thirds earned their living off the farm and used that income, along with government payments, to subsidize their operations. The failure of agricultural policy at the turn of the twenty-first century was that the federal government did not aid the farmers who needed help most.

Although the USDA and agricultural economists contended throughout much of the twentieth century that agriculture would be more efficient with fewer farmers, it was technological change that made big farms more efficient. In turn, federal farm programs gave the greatest aid to the largest and most efficient producers, because farm subsidies were linked to bushels of grain and bales of cotton rather than to the financial needs of farm families. Yet most large-scale operations were run by families who incorporated or formed partnerships for tax purposes, and still considered themselves family farmers, whether they operated 250 or 25,000 acres. The USDA considered small-scale farms to have less than $250,000 in annual sales. In 2000, farms of this size accounted for 94 percent of all farms and contributed 38 percent of the value of all agricultural production. Farmers demanded government aid, but with 10 percent of farms receiving 60 percent of price-support payments, there were considerable differences of opinion over who the farmers were and who among them deserved federal aid.

In the autumn of 2001 the House Agriculture Committee responded to the collapsing agricultural economy by writing a new farm bill that would replace the FAIR Act. It provided for $170 billion in funds over ten years, a $72 billion increase over current levels and the largest increase for any federal program, including defense. This bill abandoned congressional efforts to wean farms from government subsidies. Instead it revived earlier programs that increased crop subsidies when prices were low but reduced those payments when prices rose to target levels.

The Senate Agriculture Committee took a different approach, approving a plan called the Conservation Security Act. This bill called for the federal government to pay farmers as much as $50,000 per year for practicing soil and water conservation, and for commodity price-supporting loans. It did not require farmers to take more land out of production but would pay them for conservation work on their land. Farm-state senators were divided over the merits of the proposal, not because they opposed payments to farmers for practicing conservation, but rather because the bill did not always provide as much aid to their constituents as they wanted. It included $26.2 billion for commodity payments, for an overall program cost of $40 billion over five years, most of which would go to large-scale farmers. It also required the labeling of beef, pork, vegetables, fruits, and other foods to show country of origin. It did not limit the amount of money farmers could receive from the federal government.

The terrorist attacks of September 11, 2001, placed the new farm bills of the House and Senate in jeopardy. With new billions quickly funneled into national security and the war on

terrorists, the 2002 farm legislation soon met considerable opposition. President George W. Bush considered the House
farm bill unsatisfactory because it was too expensive, and Secretary of Agriculture Ann Veneman asked Congress to delay
consideration of a new farm bill until 2002. At least one senator suggested extending the FAIR Act by one year to gain perspective on all national expenditures, while others argued that
a new farm bill should be approved before the old one expired
in order to get as much funding as possible for farmers. When
2001 ended, Congress had failed to approve a new farm bill.
President Bush, however, pledged to support a new farm program that would provide $73.5 billion in additional spending
for various programs still in effect. This was halfway between
the House and Senate proposals. "One way or another," Secretary Veneman reported, "there will be additional spending."

She was right. Several months later, in May 2002, Congress
approved new farm legislation known as the Farm Security
and Rural Investment Act that provided $82 billion in addi-
tional spending over ten years, with increases in government
payments for major commodities based on production controls. The program recalled the Agricultural Adjustment Act
of 1938 and the Agricultural Act of 1949. The legislation also
provided payments to farmers who practiced designated soil-
conservation practices. Supporters praised the new farm legislation as an important safety net. One agricultural leader
called it "the most family farm-friendly farm bill to pass in
decades." Opponents argued that the legislation provided in-
centives for overproduction and continued to authorize large
payments only to large-scale farmers.

At the end of the twentieth century some farm organizations
boasted that the individual American farmer fed approximately 150 people, though the USDA put the figure at 103. In
reality the American farmer fed no one, not even himself.

Farmers produced a raw commodity that they sold to others for processing, and they bought their food at the grocery store just like everyone else.

Amidst national and international turmoil, a declining agricultural economy, continued decrease of the farm population, flight from the land, and the consolidation of farms, no one could say what future farm policy would be. The only certainty was that farmers and their representatives in the agricultural and commodity organizations and the agribusiness community would demand their fair share, however defined, from the federal government—without regulations if possible, but with regulations if necessary. In September 2000 Bob Stallman, president of the American Farm Bureau Federation, wrote that most of the ideas for revising agricultural policy would require "additional government money." Above all, farm supporters argued that agricultural policy needed to keep farmers on the land. Many taxpayers, however, still considered farm policy an expensive and unnecessary drain on the Treasury, ignoring the fact that it kept food abundant and prices low. By century's end, Americans spent less than 12 percent of their disposable income for food, the lowest rate in the industrialized world.

Some farmers considered the FAIR Act of 1996 satisfactory. Even though it provided for the end of price-support payments, it enabled farmers to plant without acreage restrictions, and they knew that Congress would provide emergency financial aid if the economy took a turn for the worse. But they had no desire to give up their dependence on the federal government for financial support. Rather, they favored government "green payments" for conservation practices and alternative energy development, such as ethanol and other farm-based lubricants. These payments would not limit a farmer's freedom to produce as much as possible, but they would provide an agricultural safety net.

Other farmers understood that free-market economics had been a disaster for them. They wanted to continue loan deficiency payments through the Commodity Credit Corporation, and other income-support payments that linked prices to production (similar to farm policy before the FAIR Act), even if production and marketing regulations limited their freedom of action. Livestock producers also wanted support to pay for new environmental regulations that mandated specific practices such as sewage treatment and requirements for animal confinement. Early in the twenty-first century Congress met some of these desires with new legislation that returned to the policies of the past for commodity program payments and looked to the future by providing payments for participation in conservation programs.

At century's end farmers, agricultural organizations, and farm-state politicians continued to espouse the need to save small farms, despite decades of financial evidence that showed only the larger farms were profitable. Medium-sized farms—those that most people considered family farms—barely broke even, while small farms, the most numerous, usually lost money. Considering only profitability, at the end of the century there were still too many farmers who wanted an agricultural life but who could not make enough money to enjoy a satisfactory standard of living. And this is why many farm men and women continued to leave agriculture. Others wanted to remain on the land because of their attachments to the rural past or nostalgic views of farm life, and because they believed that farm life was morally superior to life in the towns and cities, even though it was not profitable.

The pastoral image of American farming remained fixed in the minds of many farmers, and it reminded them of such virtues as independence, self-reliance, and the importance of community and common purpose. Agriculture, they argued, was an integral part of American moral and political life, an equivalent of the public good. Yet farmers' dependency on government income-support programs contradicted many of these beliefs, and many farmers continued to leave the land because they could not support their families on small-scale farms. Some critics called farmers and their organizations "competitive whiners" for "government welfare checks." Others argued that price- and income-support and environmental programs for farmers benefited the general welfare because abundant food supplies and soil conservation were essential to national security. Whoever was right, the dependency of farmers on the federal government remained a fact of life, though not everyone was happy about it, including the farmers.

A Note on Sources

READERS who are interested in a broad survey of American agricultural history should see R. Douglas Hurt, *American Agriculture: A Brief History* (Ames, Iowa, 1994). David B. Danbom focuses on rural social history in *Born in the Country: A History of Rural America* (Baltimore, 1995). John T. Schlebecker, *Whereby We Thrive: A History of American Farming, 1607–1972* (Ames, Iowa, 1975) stresses scientific and technological change. For overviews of twentieth-century American agriculture that emphasize economics, technology, and policy, see Gilbert C. Fite, *American Farmers: The New Minority* (Bloomington, Ind., 1981), and John L. Shover, *First Majority–Last Minority: The Transforming of Rural Life in America* (De Kalb, Ill., 1976). Stewart E. Tolnay provides an excellent survey of African-American farmers between 1910 and 1940 in *The Bottom Rung: African American Family Life on Southern Farms* (Urbana, Ill., 1999). See also Loren Schweninger, *Black Property Owners in the South, 1790–1915* (Urbana, Ill., 1990), and "African Americans in Southern Agriculture, 1877–1945," *Agricultural History* 72 (Spring 1998). This special issue contains twenty-one articles on African-American agriculture. For an overview of American Indian agriculture that emphasizes policy, see R. Douglas Hurt, *Indian Agriculture in America: From Prehistory to the Present* (Lawrence, Kans., 1987).

Several regional studies provide important perspectives. For the South, see Pete Daniel, *Breaking the Land: The Transformation of Cotton, Tobacco, and Rice Cultures Since 1880* (Urbana, Ill., 1986), and his "Transformation of the Rural South 1930 to the Present," *Agricultural History* 55 (July 1981), 231–248; Gilbert C. Fite, *Cotton Fields No More: Southern Agriculture, 1865–1980* (Lexington, Ky., 1984); Jack Temple Kirby, *Rural Worlds Lost:*

The American South, 1920–1960 (Baton Rouge, 1987); Donald L. Winters, "Agriculture in the Post–World War II South," in R. Douglas Hurt, ed., The Rural South Since World War II (Baton Rouge, 1998), 8–27; and Charles S. Aiken, The Cotton Plantation South Since the Civil War (Baltimore, 1998). Northern agricultural developments during the early twentieth century can be studied in Hal S. Barron, Mixed Harvest: The Second Great Transformation in the Rural North, 1870–1940 (Chapel Hill, 1999), and Mary Neth, Preserving the Family Farm: Women, Community, and the Foundations of Agribusiness in the Midwest, 1900–1940 (Baltimore, 1995). For policy implications regarding agriculture in the West, see Ellen Lieberman, California Farmland: A History of Large Agricultural Holdings (Totowa, N.J., 1983). Mark Friedberger compares family farmers in Iowa and California's Central Valley in Farm Families and Change in the Twentieth Century (Lexington, Ky., 1988).

Useful economic studies include Sally H. Clarke, Regulation and the Revolution in United States Farm Productivity (Cambridge, Mass., 1994); Marvin Duncan and Jerome M. Stam, eds., Financing Agriculture into the Twenty-First Century (Boulder, Colo., 1998); Milton C. Halberg, Economic Trends in U.S. Agriculture and Food Systems Since World War II (Ames, Iowa, 2001); and Neil E. Harl, The Farm Debt Crisis of the 1980s (Ames, Iowa, 1990). Milton C. Halberg's Policy for American Agriculture: Choices and Consequences (Ames, Iowa, 1992) surveys public policies since 1933 that deal with farm income, credit, and labor as well as food and price stability, international trade, and standardization of grading for agricultural commodities, among other considerations. See also Deborah Fitzgerald, "Accounting for Change: Farmers and the Modernizing State," in Catherine McNicol Stock and Robert D. Johnston, eds. The Countryside in the Age of the Modern State: Political Histories of Rural America (Ithaca, 2001).

Elizabeth Sanders, in Roots of Reform: Farmers, Workers, and the American State, 1877–1917 (Chicago, 1999), provides an important analysis of Progressive Era policies that affected farmers within the context of the regulatory state. Roy V. Scott evaluates the origin and development of the Extension Service in *The Reluctant Farmer: The Rise of Agricultural Extension to 1914* (Urbana, Ill., 1970). For the policy implications of the Country Life Movement, see David B. Danbom, *The Resisted Revolution: Urban America and the Industrialization of Agriculture, 1900–1930* (Ames, Iowa, 1979), and William L. Bowers, *The Country Life Movement in America, 1900–1920* (Port Washington, N.Y., 1974).

Excellent studies of agricultural policy during the 1920s and early 1930s include James H. Shideler, *Farm Crisis, 1919–1923* (Berkeley, 1957); David E. Hamilton, *From New Day to New Deal: American Farm Policy from Hoover to Roosevelt, 1928–1933* (Chapel Hill, 1991); and Philip A. Grant, Jr., "Southern Congressmen and Agriculture, 1921–1932," *Agricultural History* 53 (January 1979), 338–351. The best detailed introductions to New Deal farm programs and agriculture are Theodore Saloutos, *The American Farmer and the New Deal* (Ames, Iowa, 1982); Richard Lowitt, *The New Deal and the West* (Bloomington, Ind., 1982); and Michael W. Schuyler, *The Dread of Plenty: Agricultural Relief Activities of the Federal Government in the Middle West, 1933–1939* (Manhattan, Kans., 1989). See also R. Douglas Hurt, "Prices, Payments, & Production: Kansas Wheat Farmers and the Agricultural Adjustment Administration, 1933–1939," *Kansas History* 23 (Spring–Summer 2000), 72–87. An anti–New Deal analysis is offered by Gary Dean Best, *Pride, Prejudice, and Politics: Roosevelt Versus Recovery, 1933–1938* (New York, 1991), and by Melvyn Dubofsky and Stephen Burwood, eds., *Agriculture During the Great Depression* (New York, 1990). Richard S. Kirkendall studies the role of intellectuals in the formulation of New Deal agricultural policies in *Social Scientists and Farm Policies in the Age of Roosevelt* (Columbia, Mo., 1966). Allen J. Matusow, *Farm Policies and Politics in the Truman Years* (Cambridge, Mass., 1967) presents an overview of the Truman administration's farm problems and policies. For the significance of the farm vote in the 1948 presidential election, see Virgil Dean, "Farm Policy and Truman's 1948 Campaign," *Historian* 55 (Spring 1993), 501–516, and Thomas G. Ryan, "Farm Prices and the Farm Vote in 1948,"

Agricultural History 54 (July 1980), 387–401. For analysis of the Brannan Plan, see Virgil Dean, "The Farm Policy Debate of 1949–50: Plains State Reaction to the Brannan Plan," *Great Plains Quarterly* 13 (Winter 1993), 33–46, and "Why Not the Brannan Plan?" *Agricultural History* 70 (Spring 1996), 268–282.

Edward L. Schapsmeier and Frederick H. Schapsmeier, in "Eisenhower and Ezra Taft Benson: Farm Policy in the 1950s," *Agricultural History* 44 (October 1970), 369–378, argue that Eisenhower disapproved of the scope of governmental intervention in agriculture and chose a secretary of agriculture who reflected his farm policy views. See also their study "Farm Policy from FDR to Eisenhower: Southern Democrats and the Politics of Agriculture," *Agricultural History* 53 (January 1979), 352–371. For the Kennedy administration, see James N. Giglio, "New Frontier Agricultural Policy: The Commodity Side, 1961–1963," *Agricultural History* 61 (Summer 1987), 53–70.

"Twentieth-Century Farm Policies," *Agricultural History* 70 (Spring 1996) is a special issue that contains sixteen essays on a variety of topics from the Brannan Plan to the decision-making process in the drafting of agricultural policy. Two recent studies that look ahead as well as to the past are David Orden, Robert Paarlberg, and Terry Roe, *Policy Reform in American Agriculture: Analysis and Prognosis* (Chicago, 1999), and Robert Paarlberg and Don Paarlberg, "Agricultural Policy in the Twentieth Century," *Agricultural History* 74 (Spring 2000), 136–161.

Important evaluations of agricultural policymaking are John Mark Hansen, *Gaining Access: Congress and the Farm Lobby, 1919–1981* (Chicago, 1991), and William P. Browne, *The Failure of National Rural Policy: Institutions and Interests* (Washington, D.C., 2001). See also William P. Browne, *Cultivating Congress: Constituents, Issues, and Interests in Agricultural Policymaking* (Lawrence, Kans., 1995); William P. Browne, et al., *Sacred Cows and Hot Potatoes: Agrarian Myths in Agricultural Policy* (Boulder, Colo., 1992); and Adam D. Sheingate, "The Rise of the Agricultural Welfare State: United States Farm Policy in Historical and Comparative Perspective," (Ph.D. dissertation, Yale University,

1997). For the effect of agricultural policy on farmers in the Far West, see Thomas R. Wessel, "Agricultural Policy Since 1945," in R. Douglas Hurt, ed., *The Rural West Since World War II* (Lawrence, Kans., 1998), 76–98. Older but still useful studies of agricultural policy include Murray R. Benedict, *Farm Policies of the United States, 1790–1950* (New York, 1953), and Willard W. Cochrane and Mary E. Ryan, *American Farm Policy, 1948–1973* (Minneapolis, 1976). Luther Tweeton, in *Foundations of Farm Policy* (Lincoln, 1970), argues that farm policy must be studied in economic, social, and political perspectives. See also Ingolf Vogeler's *The Myth of the Family Farm: Agribusiness Domain of U.S. Agriculture* (Boulder, Colo., 1981).

Agricultural policy in relation to water can be studied in Norris Hundley, Jr., *Californians and Water: A History*, rev. ed. (Berkeley, 2001), and John Walton, *Western Times and Water Wars: States, Culture and Rebellion in California* (Berkeley, 1992). Donald J. Pisani has written extensively about water policy in the West; see *From Family Farm to Agribusiness: The Irrigation Crusade in the West, 1850–1931* (Berkeley, 1984); *To Reclaim a Divided West: Water Law and Public Policy, 1848–1902* (Albuquerque, 1992); *Water Land and the Law in the West: The Limits of Public Policy, 1850–1920* (Lawrence, Kans., 1996); *Water and American Government: The Reclamation Bureau, National Water Policy, and the West, 1902–1935* (Berkeley, 2002); and "Federal Water Policy and the Rural West," in, Hurt, *The Rural West Since World War II* (Lawrence, Kans., 1998), 119–146. See also "Water and Rural History," *Agricultural History* 76 (Spring 2002). This special issue contains more than two dozen articles on irrigation and water policy, primarily in the West.

Lowell K. Dyson provides a useful guide to agricultural groups in *Farmers' Organizations* (New York, 1986). For a brief summary of agricultural organizations, see Patrick H. Mooney and Theo J. Majka, *Farmers' and Farm Workers' Movements: Social Protest in American Agriculture* (New York, 1995). Cindy Hahamovitch provides an excellent study of migrant labor along the east coast in *The Fruits of Their Labor: Atlantic Coast Farmwork-*

ers and the Making of Migrant Poverty, 1870–1945 (Chapel Hill, 1997). For studies that emphasize the West, see J. Craig Jenkins, *The Politics of Insurgency: The Farm Worker Movement of the 1960s* (Columbia, Mo., 1985); Cletus E. Daniel, *Bittersweet Harvest: A History of California Farmworkers, 1870–1941* (Ithaca, 1981); Mark Reisler, *By the Sweat of Their Brow: Mexican Migrant Labor in the United States, 1900–1941* (Westport, Conn., 1976); Emilio Zamora, *The World of Mexican Workers in Texas* (College Station, Tex., 1993); and Neil Foley, *White Scourge: Mexicans, Blacks, and Poor Whites in Texas Cotton Culture* (Berkeley, 1997). See also Theodore Saloutos and John D. Hicks, *Agricultural Discontent in the Middle West, 1900–1939* (Madison, Wisc., 1951). For the South, see Theodore Saloutos, *Farmer Movements in the South, 1865–1933* (Berkeley, 1960), and "Agricultural Organizations and Farm Policy in the South After World War II," *Agricultural History* 53 (January 1979), 377–404.

Important introductions to the history of agribusiness include Harry C. McDean, "Agribusiness in the American West," in Hurt, *The Rural West Since World War II* (Lawrence, Kans., 1998), 231–244, and the studies of Wayne G. Broehl, Jr., *Cargill: Going Global* (Hanover, N.H., 1998); *Cargill: Trading the World's Grain* (Hanover, N.H., 1992); and *John Deere's Company: A History of Deere & Company and Its Times* (New York, 1984). See also Ernesto Galaraza, *Farm Workers and Agri-Business in California* (South Bend, Ind., 1977), and "Agribusiness and International Agriculture: The New Farmers," *Agricultural History* 69 (Spring 1995). This special issue contains fourteen articles on the history of agribusiness.

The importance of technological change in twentieth-century American agriculture can be traced in R. Douglas Hurt, *Agricultural Technology in the Twentieth Century* (Manhattan, Kans., 1991); Donald R. Holley, *The Second Great Emancipation: The Mechanical Cotton Picker, Black Migration, and How They Shaped the Modern South* (Fayetteville, Ark., 2000); J. Sanford Rikoon, *Threshing in the Midwest, 1820–1940: A Study of Traditional Culture and Technological Change* (Bloomington, Ind., 1988); Robert

C. Williams, *Fordson, Farmall, and Poppin' Johnny: A History of the Farm Tractor and Its Impact on America* (Urbana, Ill., 1987); Thomas D. Isern, *Custom Combining on the Great Plains: A History* (Norman, Okla., 1981); William H. Friedland, *Green Gold: Capital, Labor, and Technology in the Lettuce Industry* (Cambridge, Mass., 1981); and Judith Fabry, "Agricultural Science and Technology in the West," in Hurt, *The Rural West Since World War II* (Lawrence, Kans., 1998), 169–189.

Index

A NOTE ON THE AUTHOR

R. Douglas Hurt directs the graduate program in agricultural history and rural studies at Iowa State University, and is editor of the journal *Agricultural History.* He studied at Fort Hays State University and received a Ph.D. from Kansas State University. He has also written *American Agriculture: A Brief History, American Farm Tools, Agricultural Technology in the Twentieth Century, American Farms,* and *The Dust Bowl,* among other books. He lives in Ames, Iowa.